STOP THE PRESSES

RICHARD S. LEVICK, ESQ.
AND LARRY SMITH

STOP THE PRESSES

The Crisis and Litigation PR Desk Reference

SECOND EDITION

FOREWORD BY

JACK TROUT

THE WORLD'S FOREMOST MARKETING STRATEGIST

© 2007 by Richard S. Levick and Larry Smith

All Rights Reserved.

Second Edition, December 2007

Published by:

WATERSHED PRESS
1900 M Street, NW
Washington, DC 20036

Stop the Presses was originally published by
Levick Strategic Communications, LLC in 2004.

Designed by Rock Creek Strategic Marketing.
Printed in the United States of America.

Library of Congress Cataloging-in-Publication Data has been applied for.
ISBN: 978-0-9759985-2-6

Contents

STOP THE PRESSES

The Crisis and Litigation PR Desk Reference

SECOND EDITION

Bullet-Proofing Your Brand

As much as anyone, you could say that I have a vested interest in this book.

My career has been devoted to helping companies build brands. Now, brands are by definition multifaceted. They literally infuse everything a company does, from how it makes its products or delivers its services, to how it sells those products or services. Marketing, which is where strategists like myself get involved, are either tied directly to the brand or they're useless.

Brands are built over time and become recognizable entities in their marketplace. Nothing is more important in the evolution of a brand than the trustworthiness it communicates. A brand tells the public that it can rely on a product being safe or that dependable service will be delivered with a smile. Reputation and brand are not exactly synonymous but they are inseparable.

So of what lasting value would our work be if all that brand capital, which is the basis of effective marketing, were to disappear in a virtual instant?

If you give something of value to someone, you expect them to take good care of it. Unfortunately, we live in a dangerous world. There is hardly a single business entity out there that is not susceptible to a devastating assault, fair or not. You can spend decades building a brand only to have it face relentless public attack in the mere time it takes for one reporter to file a story or for one blogger to fulminate online.

Stop the Presses: The Crisis and Litigation PR Handbook is all about how to prevent that from happening. It is about building and rebuilding brands by going on the offense, not only with marketing, but, at the earliest opportunity, with preparation to face the challenges ahead. You can therefore understand why I feel this is an important book. Professionals like Richard Levick and Larry Smith are the necessary complement to strategists like me. They've been salvaging reputations and rescuing brands for decades now. This book distills the wisdom they've gained as a result. As you read it, I advise that you think beyond protecting your brand. More than that, I advise you to think, as they would say, *bullet-proof your brand!*

It is, to be sure, a tall order in a world that has become such a minefield. The public distrusts business as never before. Attitudes, once formed, harden pretty quickly. Your competitors may secretly encourage attacks against you. Yet take the lessons in *Stop the Presses* to heart and you'll see how bullet-proofing your brand is a realistic as well as a necessary goal.

At a basic level, bullet-proofing your brand means knowing how and when to get into the news, and it means knowing how and when to get out of the news. In the first instance, brand preservation requires you to say something to the world and to say it effectively. It may be after you've been attacked or a problem has been disclosed, or it may be in anticipation of disclosure. By speaking ahead of the crisis, you inoculate yourself against the bacteria. As the authors like to put it, "run *to* the crisis."

In the second instance, discretion is the much better part of valor. As Richard and Larry show, there's something called a "Don't Panic Button." Reporters may be calling. The birds of prey may be hovering. But even then there are ways to bullet-proof your brand. You can minimize the bad story. Sometimes you can kill it altogether.

Yet brand protection is not just a simple matter of shrewd press relations. It is a campaign in the truest sense. It happens online and off. The tools at your disposal are innumerable and you'll find the most important ones enumerated in these pages. You'll learn how to integrate those weapons into a crisis communications program at three critical junctures.

First, before a crisis happens. Plan for crises that may never happen. Never stop thinking about what could realistically confront you someday, whether it's Sarbanes-Oxley or a product recall. Know who the bloggers are as well as the politicians and regulators. Build on the trust you already have with your customers and in your community. The trust bank can never be big enough.

Businesses buy fire insurance without questioning its value. Why question the value of prophylactic crisis planning that provides equally critical insurance for your brand and reputation? With planning comes training. Are your key executives equipped to respond to a fire alarm? In today's transparent marketplace, they ought to be.

Second, during a crisis. There are unique aspects to every crisis but there are also universally applicable best practices. Human beings learn from the experiences of other human beings; industries learn from the experience of other industries. There's a wealth of example in this book of what companies have done right and what they've done wrong during crises. Each one is a learning experience for the reader.

Third, after a crisis. Bullet-proofing your brand doesn't mean that some temporary damage won't be done. Reporters will be unfair. Customers will defect. But reporters can be won over and customers can be won back. The end of a crisis is merely the cue for new efforts to reaffirm and strengthen the brand—perhaps to a point where it is even stronger than before the crisis occurred.

At each juncture, you need an Internet strategy. You need to be as fast as a keystroke in how you communicate online. As we learn in *Stop the Presses*, it's never enough to simply post a website. You need to have a rapid-response capacity so that you can anticipate, prepare, and defend. You need an "optimization" strategy to ensure maximum online readership. Optimization is, in fact, so important that Richard and Larry have devoted a whole new chapter to it in this new edition of their book.

The second edition of *Stop the Presses*, with its new material on blogs, on food recalls, on data security breaches, on boardroom melees, shows just how much has happened in the three years since it was first published. Events are spiraling, seemingly beyond control. But you need to control them. You need to master them.

If you don't, it could be good night and good luck.

—Jack Trout

Jack Trout is President of Trout & Partners, one of the most prestigious marketing firms in the United States, with offices in 21 countries and a client list that includes AT&T, IBM, Merrill Lynch, Southwest Airlines and the U.S. State Department. Recognized as one of the influential gurus of marketing, Trout was the first to popularize the idea of "positioning" products and ideas in the minds of consumers. A sought-after speaker, he is the author of numerous marketing classics including the bestselling Positioning: The Battle for Your Mind, The 22 Immutable Laws of Marketing, *and 1998's* The Power of Simplicity.

Things Change,
Things Stay the Same

When the first edition of *Stop the Presses* was published, the network news anchors were Tom Brokaw, Peter Jennings, and Dan Rather. Gas cost a little over a buck a gallon. Apple was still working out the kinks in something called an iPod. Not many CEOs worried about personal liability in corporate dealings unless they actually were crooks. The concept of the "blogosphere" was in its infancy.

A few short years later, Brian Williams, Charles Gibson, and Katie Couric are anchoring the network news. In the days of Brokaw, Jennings, and Rather, a corporation under fire would typically have one day to respond to allegations. These days, a full day's delay can have a catastrophic effect on stock values.

The cost of gas has skyrocketed. Some households have two or three iPods each with no apparent end in sight. Because of a barrage of scandals, every corporation in America must now comply with the strict dictates of Sarbanes-Oxley, while more than a few CEOs endure sleepless nights worrying about personal exposure.

Hundreds of thousands of people worldwide blog and "plog," which is a close variant on blog standing for "personalized web log." They do it every day. Some do it because it's fun and educational. Some because they have a mission or agenda, and some because they have greedy or sinister aims.

We can only guess at the profound changes—economic, legal, political, technological, and cultural—that will take place between now and the third edition of *Stop the Presses*. But it's guaranteed that those changes will come and it's your job, as well as ours, to monitor and manage their effects on our brands, companies, and governments. Strengths and vulnerabilities, risks and opportunities, must be strategically assessed. Responsive initiatives must be implemented.

In the world of crisis management and litigation communications, change is the only constant. The rules of engagement are perpetually evolving. Corporations and institutions adapt to those changes or else their exposure is incalculable. Woe betide any organization caught unprepared or flatfooted by a consumer boycott or a class action lawsuit or a hostile grassroots campaign. Not just companies and high-profile individuals, but whole countries are susceptible to incessant and protracted online blandishments.

Yet, if there is one single change that justifies a second edition of this book, it's the sea change in Internet communications that now ties the world's most powerful corporations to the humblest public interest groups in an unholy dance of "Gotcha" and "Gotcha Back." As such, we have added new chapters that deal specifically with strategies like blogging as well as persistently unheralded but monumentally effective tactics like "Search Engine Optimization." Such concepts and tactics were still on the launching pad (if that) when *Stop the Presses* was originally published.

Think for a minute about how technology has transformed the way we work and interact. Hand-held devices—primed not only to send and receive information instantaneously, but to take motion pictures and still photographs—used to be a fairly exclusive device provided for select senior executives. Now they're a near-ubiquitous tool of mid- and even entry-level employees. They're also in the hands of investigative reporters, crusading activists, and sometimes just a passerby who serendipitously captures the unforgettable "gotcha" moment for the visual record. Everybody today buys ink by the barrel.

Blogging was, until recently, the almost-exclusive province of college students and technophiles. Now, it's an absolutely essential source of information on potential trouble for every kind of corporation as well as a way to market its own goods and services. Blogs are also the most cost-effective way for the plaintiffs' bar to recruit class litigants.

Even today, SEO (i.e., Search Engine Optimization) remains a relatively obscure concept, even to many communications professionals. Among Internet professionals, however, it is now a basic tool. Those who use this tool for any number of online purposes enjoy a powerful advantage over their adversaries and competitors. For example, many more activists have figured out ways to optimize their presence on the Internet and thereby guarantee wider visibility and credibility for their causes. A $5 billion company that does not optimize its online resources will likely be bested online by their critics who may not even be spending six figures. Optimization is as cost-effective as it is powerful.

For this second edition, we have incorporated chapters on these seismic Internet changes in order to flesh out their essential implications for corporate and institutional communicators. In light of stepped-up regulatory activity, we have also included substantial new content on dealing with regulators, and we've taken a fresh look at how related issues affect the food and pharmaceutical industries.

At the same time, the fundamental best practices of crisis communications that originally engaged our readers (to an extent, if we may say, happily beyond our own expectations) are still substantially relevant. As such, many of our original chapters, updated for this edition, merit the attention of board members, C-Suite managers, lawyers, and, of course, communications professionals—perhaps even more so today, in fact, as the stakes ratchet up as never before.

Crisis team formation and crisis planning, for example, are no less essential than three years ago. The media response cycle is more exigent than three years ago as online global media increasingly dominate. Today, being prepared is critical to an extent that is truly unprecedented. Judgment is nearly instantaneous, often unforgiving, and increasingly permanent, sometimes with consequences in the criminal as well as civil justice system. The penalties for ostrich-like denial are more severe, while the companies and institutions at risk are more numerous than at any other time in American history.

The common wisdom of crisis management and litigation communications has only been reinforced in the first decade of the 21st century. It is still a potentially fatal misstep to ignore or "no comment" a reporter who's gathering background or, to be sure, already on deadline. In the casting of most stories, the media still assigns crucial and predictable roles: public malefactor, sympathetic target, or socially responsible hero. From a business standpoint, your bottom line is still decisively affected by which role you play and how well you play it.

Lawyers are sometimes part of the problem and sometimes part of the solution. Too many outside counsel unfortunately still regard public communications as a risk that is never really worth taking. On the defense side, lawyers who understand the impact of public opinion, and are capable of affecting it, are rare, especially when their clients are corporations.

The plaintiffs' bar, on the other hand, views communications as a veritable full employment act. Trial attorneys as well as regulators and NGOs are masterful media manipulators and they're getting better at it all the time. Companies, countries, high net worth individuals, and other targets need to match their savvy and intensity.

A few years ago, Daimler/Chrysler commissioned research about how the consuming public was likely to react in a crisis situation with *no* facts, yet still confronted with the question, "Is the company guilty or innocent?" The data gathered was sobering. More than two-thirds of consumers presumed companies to be guilty simply because they were accused, the absence of facts notwithstanding. It's the people who buy your products that are most predisposed to find you guilty as charged.

In the face of such odds, businesses, governments and others afflicted have only one choice: to anticipate, prepare, and, when confronted, fight back, honestly and resolutely. *Stop the Presses* is a battle plan in a war you cannot afford to lose.

Richard S. Levick, Esq.
Larry Smith

ONE

The Life Cycle of A Brand

It's March 18, 2007, a crisp and sunny Sunday morning. Ah yes, *The New York Times*…So, what's fit to print today?

Front page, bottom left column headline: "Airlines Learn to Fly on a Wing and an Apology." It seems that Southwest has a guy named Fred Taylor Jr. whose whole job is uncovering things about his employer's performance to apologize for—and then writing "folksy" letters to all the passengers who were inconvenienced.

The Times dubs Taylor the "Chief Apology Officer," emphasizing that the whole program, in place now for five years, directly reflects the personality of Southwest president Colleen Barrett. A smiley photograph of Taylor with Barrett confirms the affinity.

It's called *brand equity*. In this case, the brand is defined in part as the unstinted concern of an American corporation with the welfare and happiness of its customers. Southwest built that brand years ago—and what's telling here is that they're still pulling out all stops to continue building it.

To be sure, Southwest is one of the remarkable brand management examples in recent history. Consider the revolutionary impact of a company promoting the fact that it offers no frills whatsoever. It is diametrically opposed to how most companies sell products and services, yet, as of this writing, passengers are around five to ten times more likely to recommend Southwest than the major airlines.

The power of a brand is to enlist millions as an unpaid sales force.

Equally important, this specific brand identity directly apprehends the kind of crisis that nearly sunk JetBlue on February 14, 2007 when that airline's stranded passengers fought a virtual pitched battle with beleaguered and increasingly hostile employees. As cultural valence, Southwest's apology program is the essence of crisis preparedness at the most strategic level.

At the tactical level, preparedness requires templates for action —whom to contact, what to say, which resources to deploy and how. But there's more to preparedness than process.

There is also the fund of goodwill from which customers and other key audiences can draw when a crisis does occur. A person who receives a letter of apology because his or her flight was cancelled due to a mechanical malfunction will be significantly more understanding a few months later when a national ice storm savages flight patterns everywhere.

Southwest's apology program thus defines the critical dovetailing of brand development and crisis preparedness. Of course, there's no guarantee that the fund of goodwill won't be quickly depleted were Southwest to suffer the same sort of systemic breakdown that happened to JetBlue. But capital in the bank is better than no capital in the bank—and the fact that JetBlue had taken its own powerful steps, not unlike what Southwest historically accomplished, proves the value of brand equity during a crisis. All brands face crisis sometimes, and vigilant companies never view their brands as impervious to public attacks. Quite to the contrary, it's to withstand such attacks that the brands are built and nurtured.

It's not a simple process. In fact, it can be a dangerous one as JetBlue's ordeal and ultimate triumph demonstrate.

Much of the media coverage around the JetBlue crisis reminded the public that the company's problem directly contradicted its brand. In that sense, the brand identity was actually a liability because JetBlue seemed unable to keep a promise. Brands, whether based on customer care or product reliability, are nothing more or less than promises. Break one promise, lose a customer. Break enough promises and you're out of business.

Promises are therefore not enough. You need systems in place to make sure they're kept.

Yet, the brand promise cuts two ways. As reports of the Jet-Blue debacle circulated, many passengers were also saying, "Hold on, those flight cancellations and runway delays aren't the airline I know. Maybe there's a reason why this breakdown occurred."

In fact, as soon as David Neeleman, JetBlue's founder and CEO, made the media rounds apologizing and reaffirming JetBlue's commitment—even formalizing a passenger's bill of rights one big step ahead of a similar initiative before Congress—the power of the brand reasserted itself. The sheer frequency with which he appeared in the media underscored his own personal consciousness that a promise had been broken, that that was unacceptable, and that practical steps would have to be taken to guarantee that the bill of rights would be enforced. People were willing to believe Neeleman in a way that they would not have believed....well, Frank Lorenzo, for one.

When it comes to crisis, your brand is a responsibility, it is an asset, it is an insurance policy, it is a burden, and it is also an opportunity.

EVER VIGILANT

As the link between brand and crisis, the media obviously plays its greatest part during the crisis itself when there are breaking events to report as well as an opportunity to reflect (as certainly happened in the coverage of JetBlue) on the relationship between those vexatious events and the culture of the organizations involved.

That said, all marketing is a form of crisis preparedness because it defines the brand at every stage of development. No specific crisis compelled Southwest to hire a Chief Apology Officer, and no specific crisis convinced *The New York Times* to run a feature article about Mr. Taylor. Yet Mr. Taylor is no less an effective guardian of the Southwest brand, and the article about him is an arrow in the company's crisis management arsenal if only because it's proof positive that Southwest works hard to prevent crises before they happen.

The need to "think crisis"—crisis preparedness and crisis response—during the entire life cycle of a brand is underscored by the fact that, as research by PricewaterhouseCoopers confirms, 49%, or virtually one-half, of U.S.-based multinationals have faced crises in the last three years. It's called the "success tax." As a company grows, it becomes notable, and notable in a way that highlights its deep pockets or incites those who, for one reason or another, are suspicious of the success.

Many of those crises are of the bet-the-company variety, especially at a time when government oversight has imposed such extraordinary burdens on public companies. Sarbanes-Oxley is just one example but right now the most dramatic one. At a March 2007 Treasury Department conference on market competitiveness, former Treasury secretary Robert Rubin warned that, if he were a CEO, he'd be "scared to death" to certify his company's financial results. "[F]ive years down the road," the CEO may be held liable for myriad omissions or asked to explain some then-innocuous digression.

As a result, there is additional reason to think in terms of crisis preparedness and crisis response at all stages of the brand development process. It is, as we've seen, a positive, goodwill-building process that creates assets to draw on when the bad-case scenarios happen. On the other hand, you also need to "think crisis" throughout the brand life cycle because every decision you make—every accounting certification, every marketing choice—may eventually be questioned by a regulator, a journalist, an analyst, a shareholder. Today's best-faith compliance efforts or product safety initiatives may, as circumstances evolve, seem woefully inadequate or even dishonest in the years ahead. Ask Merck about the internal decisions made during the manufacturing and marketing of Vioxx, and if those decisions were ever expected to spawn one of the monumental litigation events of the century.

You cannot erase past mistakes, but you can start making decisions as if there were a *60 Minutes* camera in the boardroom. There's no calling back yesterday's injudicious emails but you can institutionalize new systems to minimize such indiscretions in the future. And, you should start planning as if yesterday's mistakes will in fact come to light at any time.

As we will discuss in subsequent chapters, such planning means forming crisis teams and crisis plans. But the company cannot be satisfied with just that. Typically, plans and templates are created, then housed in the computers of the legal and communications departments, and then largely forgotten after they're officially approved.

Preparedness means more. It requires periodic training for media crises along with crisis fire drills. At the very least, such hands-on training keeps the crisis team primed and ready to deploy. It keeps the human interaction among team members alive and, internally, it builds trust over time even as it provides a forum for lively and practical new ideas.

Preparation and planning also mean the ability to act at a second's notice. Today's world requires a rapid-response Internet strategy. Armed with the foresight to identify the kinds of crises your company may face, you can, for example, have any number of possible "dark sites" ready to deploy online when they're needed. These sites are fully formatted and already include basic statements in support of your anticipated position. You then fill in the details and post live, ideally before the first story has run in the daily paper.

Internet readiness means constantly monitoring the online initiatives of potential adversaries as well, before there's a crisis in sight. During the 2006 spinach E.coli scare, activists and food industry adversaries went immediately online with their attacks (see Chapter 9). They clearly had their technology and crisis templates ready to activate. All they needed was to fill in the words "spinach," "California," "E.coli," etc. once the details of the crisis were known.

(Continued on page 8)

A View from the Boardroom:
Obligation plus Liability Equals Involvement

Although it's not a board's mission or responsibility to manage a company, the strategic oversight that independent directors can provide is increasingly important across a range of issues—and nowhere more tangibly than in times of crisis.

Not surprisingly, the Sarbanes-Oxley Act of 2002 increased the burden on directors because it mandated that only independent directors with no affiliation to the companies they serve could sit on certain board committees. This measure not only gave boards more independence, but more responsibility—and liability—as well.

For example, in a banner class-action lawsuit against World-Com led by the New York State Common Retirement Fund, the telecommunications giant's independent directors were ruled negligent and *personally* liable for a portion of the company's losses. This outcome reinforced the serious nature and potential consequences of their duties and catalyzed new awareness of the greater crisis management roles that they would now have to play.

Today, board members have three overriding concerns about how companies handle crisis communications, according to Lawrence P. English, Chairman of Lawrence P. English & Associates, a crisis and turnaround management firm based in Sarasota, Florida.

First, is the company telling the truth?

Second, has it complied with all SEC disclosure requirements? As an example of material information that falls through the cracks for one reason or another, English points to the May, 2007 announcement by the SEC that Hewlett-Packard Co. erred by failing to disclose why one of its directors, Thomas Perkins, resigned last year during the company's boardroom leak investigation. Although the SEC did not fine H-P, it was—after all the controversy beleaguering the company—a significant omission as Perkins' concerns were related to the company's corporate governance and policies and, by law, therefore needed to be disclosed.

Third, English articulates a very specific and practicable testing mechanism: Are company managers and directors telling shareholders what they would want to know if *they* were shareholders?

Best boardroom practices vary depending on size, says English who in the last four decades has served a broad variety of companies. He held several senior management positions at CIGNA Corporation and served as Chairman and CEO of Quadramed Corporation. He was also a director of three public companies and three private companies.

Board members should, for example, press for formal crisis preparedness but take company size and resources into careful consideration. "At CIGNA, we had a fully trained PR staff as well as outside agencies ready to step in when a crisis arose. On the other hand, at QuadraMed and other small cap companies, the Board and management need ongoing relationships with outside firms that are generally familiar with the business and skilled in crisis management, and that can be called on quickly in a crisis. These need to be real partnerships."

At one company English served as an independent director, stock prices declined after the CEO was terminated. Just weeks before, however, the Chairman of the Board had sold a large number of shares at the higher price. The fact that the Chairman had been a short seller in a previous life only threatened to fuel the incipient fire.

It was, to be sure, the kind of crisis scenario to which many small public companies are susceptible—and, says English, precisely why outside communications counsel can be as important for smaller companies as outside legal counsel. In the example English cites, the company's "partnership" with a communications firm spared it litigation and regulatory action.

Such cases underscore a critical need for directors to at least be able to identify where internal resources are deficient and must be supplemented by outside expertise. It's not just smaller companies that suffer deficiencies. When Jerry Levin became CEO of what was then Sunbeam Corp. in the late 1990s, he was surprised at how little the board knew about the very accounting problem that was then roiling the corporate waters. There was likewise a dearth of bankruptcy expertise among HealthSouth Corp. directors in the post-Richard Scrushy period that protracted the discussion of whether or not to even seek bankruptcy protection.

Such cases signal a need to elect outside directors in the same way that companies assign crisis teams—with abiding intent to cover all bases and anticipate multifaceted contingencies. In turn, directors should be given the training they need in order to perform their augmented roles.

(Continued from page 5)

In response, companies can ensure that their own sites and blogs are fully "optimized" to ensure maximum online prominence. Companies should also know well in advance who the "high-authority" bloggers are, for it's on those blogs that a crucial and perhaps decisive war of words will play out. Know which ones will give you a fair chance to make your case, and be prepared to make that case either by posting comments directly or, as is always effective, by having supportive and ostensibly disinterested third parties do so.

While plaintiffs, regulators, and NGOs have the online advantage right now, the Internet may be the best thing that has happened to corporations in terms of crisis readiness. Because it's so obviously an expanding 24/7 medium, the Internet deprives companies of any excuse for lassitude or for holding on to the foolish assumption that only an impending crisis merits crisis preparedness.

THE NEW LEADERS

In this daunting world of permanent crisis, a new breed of leaders is emerging. To understand who they are, it's first important to state who they are not. *They are not spin doctors.* They do not rely on glibness. They are not foolish enough to think they can talk their way out of what they have acted their way into.

Today's new leaders have integrity in the most fundamental sense of the word. *Integrity is doing the right thing when no one is watching.* It is an invaluable asset once someone does start watching.

Like Colleen Barrett at Southwest, leaders believe in who they are and what they do. But, also like Colleen Barrett, they know that systems go down, ice storms won't stop, and people get angry. They know that mistakes happen. They also know that even the greatest organizations may have disruptive employees and, too often, dishonest executives.

Today, leadership is all about building brand assets by speaking truthfully, preparing for the worst, and finding a way to somehow keep the promises inherent in the corporate brands. Today's leaders can only lead if they accept, as an inescapable part of their job descriptions, that they will indeed be scrutinized like fish in a tank by private interests as well as public sector overseers.

As one of those watchdogs, the media, especially as it now includes the bloggers, is important at every stage of the brand's life cycle because it is obviously the most direct conduit to other watchdogs: regulators and prosecutors, shareholders, employees, customers and clients. Implicit throughout this book, in our discussions of how media skills apply to specific industries and specific controversies, are best practices that—more than facile tools for talking to the press—speak directly to integrity and leadership as prerequisites for brand-building and crisis preparedness.

Let's make a few of these implicit best practices explicit.

- Defendants explain. Leaders narrate. Explanations sound like excuses or efforts to bury the real issue in detail. Instead, leaders describe the steps they've taken, and the steps they're going to take to solve the problem. That's what audiences want, and it's what they deserve.

- Leaders have great timing. They recognize the teachable moments when their messages will have maximum impact and they don't let those moments pass them by.

- Leaders go beyond what's expected. If consumers are waiting for an apology, leaders go further and provide a full-blown bill of rights. If regulators want information, leaders provide more than what the law requires.

- Leaders know that being leaders makes them targets. They don't recriminate or hide from the glare. They are willing to talk to hostile reporters if there is any possibility that those reporters can be won over or at least be persuaded to balance their coverage.

- Leaders build on their victories without gloating or disparaging the losers. They're successful people who make it easy for people, including reporters, to be glad about their further successes.

- Leaders know when to go on the offense. They also know how to go on the offense, usually via surrogates.

- Leaders insist on hearing bad news all at once. If possible, they insist on telling it all at once as well.

It's true that today's media crucible is unremitting and unforgiving as never before. Yet it's also a battlefield where leaders with real integrity stand the best chance of winning, simply because they are leaders and do have integrity.

So Don't Forget...

- Crisis preparedness is part and parcel of the brand-building process at every stage. It's the goodwill you generate today as an insurance policy for tomorrow's controversies.

- "Own" the Internet so that reporters, customers, analysts, and activists see your story first and often.

- Systemic preparation ensures that the promise of your brand can be kept. It includes periodic media training and crisis rehearsals. It includes constant Internet monitoring and supportive Internet resources "optimized" to ensure maximum readership.

- Explain as little as you can. Audiences want assurances, not excuses. Don't worry about them understanding intricate fact patterns that may be decisive in a court of law. In the Court of Public Opinion, when you're explaining, you're losing.

- Go beyond what's expected. To win back disappointed audiences, surprise them with something that they don't feel you necessarily owe them.

- Some stories will always be negative. Have an alternative story to tell: positive, equally impressive, equally important.

TWO

What's at Stake? Here's the Quick Answer...Maybe Everything

I t is true that the public has a short memory. It is likewise true that yesterday's blaring headlines are tomorrow's footnotes. Bad press is as ephemeral as good press. Unfortunately, the effects of that bad press can be permanent.

Negative press coverage can sabotage stock values. It can torpedo litigation strategies. People may forget the actual scandal or setback that led to a corporate, institutional, or personal crisis. But that's cold comfort if it costs you customers you may never recover, or gets you beaten in a lawsuit.

Indeed, litigation offers the most convincing examples of what's at stake, simply because media coverage may directly affect the outcome, even under the best of circumstances. Assume we can effectively isolate a jury from all contact with the media. Assume the judge is above being influenced by anything he or she reads in the newspaper. Even with those advantages, why lead with your chin? If there is not a likelihood of press coverage, generating press coverage might be the dumbest thing you can do. William Sampson, a partner at Shook, Hardy & Bacon, L.L.P., recalls a "good Kansas lawyer" who avoided talking with the press because "he knew his judge would rather hear the story first from him than from the newspaper."

Even without press coverage, there may still be a climate of opinion swirling around the case that affects the actions and decisions on both sides. Especially when the stakes are high, hidden agendas are often at play, and those agendas are usually driven not only by what happens in court, but by how the public perceives the issues. Those perceptions can determine if a case even gets to court.

Let's take a look at two very direct, and very different, examples of how media management decisively affected high-stakes litigation. As different as these cases are, they both show what invariably happens when parties to a dispute appreciate the impact of media and the importance of managing media, and what invariably happens when they don't.

> "What seems like a frivolous case becomes something else entirely when other attorneys see it discussed as a serious substantive matter in a responsible publication," advises Sandy Mc-Math, who has pioneered cases against the media once thought impossible to win.

THE REAL AGENDA

Media management related to litigation is never more important than in situations where the actual goal of the litigation is to influence the media itself in order to force public opinion in one direction or another. The purpose of some lawsuits is to inspire new legislation. Some litigants file suits to dramatize inequities. Class actions are often all about social policy, not points of law.

Under such circumstances, it behooves the other side to grasp what the hidden agenda really is. A comprehensive case strategy in these cases includes, perforce, media relations. The lawyers must work with other professionals because the client's welfare demands so much else besides legal expertise.

In the post-9/11 environment, a 1996 imbroglio speaks volumes.

One day that year, a hotel franchiser with six hotels under his wing was shocked to learn that he was being sued for discriminating against a Muslim. He was caught totally off guard with no media team, no media plan, and absolutely nothing to say in his defense. Meanwhile, the news cycles, in print and on television, were spinning dizzily. It was a hot story because it was unusual, and because the hotel chain is a brand-name outfit that would attract and keep audience interest.

An outside media team was hired, almost in desperation. Because the story had progressed so far, the PR advisors had to work through the night to get up to speed, devising responses to the allegations and crafting an overriding media strategy. Such a strategy would have to somehow trump the negative messages appearing in editorials and on TV over a seemingly interminable five-day period.

The media team took a good look at the plaintiff's attorney. They read between the lines of his public utterances and scrutinized the kind of media opportunities he was pursuing. It was soon pretty clear that this lawyer had bigger fish to fry than simply negotiating a settlement or even winning a verdict.

In fact, he saw the case as the Islamic equivalent of *Brown v. Board of Education,* as it would spotlight the often uncertain place of Muslims and Muslim-Americans in American society.

The media plan would thus have to address that larger agenda. Without such a plan, even the most effective and direct responses to the specific allegations would fall short of what had to be the real goal, which was to prevent the hotels from becoming a symbol of a larger social inequity.

The plan that was evolved amid the media maelstrom called for an outreach to the Islamic community that would have nothing directly to do with the allegations against the hotel—as was appropriate, since the allegations themselves were not the real stake in the matter.

(Continued on page 17)

What's at Stake: The Loyalty of Major Clients

Lawyers make a decisive mistake when they ignore or glibly underestimate the demand by major clients that they develop and aggressively apply media relations and crisis management skills.

Consider DaimlerChrysler. This global giant insists, not requests, that outside counsel demonstrate just such skills as a crucial component of case strategy.

"We expect our lawyers to understand some fundamental business principles, not the least of which is that the damage to a company's reputation after a case is over can far exceed, in actual dollars, the costs of the lawsuit itself," says Steven Hantler, assistant general counsel for government and regulation.

In fact, in the late 1990s, DaimlerChrysler "institutionalized" proactive media relations after the company was caught short in the press following an adverse judgment. According to Hantler, the corporation "directly and formally" advised its law firms that they would need to participate on the media end of their cases as either spokespersons or strategists or both. Some firms were "skeptical, even resistant," says Hantler. Others, like Gibson, Dunn & Crutcher, enthusiastically rose to the occasion and have continued to support the client's commitment to communicate its side of every story.

"We realized that plaintiffs' attorneys were aggressively drawing first blood in the media, and that their attacks often went unanswered," says Hantler. "We simply made it unacceptable, in many cases, for any of our lawyers to respond to those attacks with a 'no comment.' We were no longer interested in ceding the [media] field to our opponents."

Hantler believes that, with most corporate litigation, the press prefers to talk to in-house counsel. But there is certainly a role for DaimlerChrysler's outside lawyers to comment on the record as well.

At the very least, law firms must participate in all relevant media strategy sessions at DaimlerChrysler "to help us project the trajectory of case-related issues and how those issues will likely play out in the press in the months or years ahead," says Hantler.

Ideally, outside counsel will so warm to the task that they will adapt the beneficial effects to their trial strategies. In other words, DaimlerChrysler wants lawyers who instinctively understand that the message points they need to develop will have the same impact in court as in the media.

After all, the audience is really the same in both instances.

(Continued from page 15)

The solution was for the hotel's legal counsel to call a leading Islamic-American public interest group and offer a wide range of services to the Islamic community. The public interest group was delighted with the offer and disengaged from the hotel chain controversy. It was convinced that the defendant was sincere in his demonstration of good will. There would be no public castigation of the hotel franchiser or the chain, not from this key interest group.

Instant media training of the hotel franchiser, heretofore a reluctant and shy spokesperson, followed by television appearances with a heartfelt mea culpa, made the story disappear within 24 hours.

WHAT TO DO, WHAT NOT TO DO

Simpler cases mandate simpler media-relations lessons. One potentially devastating libel case offers a fundamental example of common sense in media relations. It is a compelling reminder to respect the media, and to bear in mind how badly the media can hurt you if you do not.

In 1997, a plaintiff's attorney in Little Rock named Sandy Mc-Math contacted a small-circulation, now-defunct newsletter, *Inside*

Litigation, with a case that no one else was covering, at least not at that point. It was a libel suit against the publishing companies Grove/Atlantic, Inc. and Penguin Books USA Inc., and it was a hot enough story for the editor at *Inside Litigation* to jump all over.

It concerned *Land of Opportunity*, a book that covered the careers of four brothers and how they grew up to become notorious drug dealers. The book depicted their mother, Hazel Chambers, as a prostitute, although there was no evidence whatsoever to support that characterization.

McMath patiently explained the details of his case to the *Inside Litigation* reporter without being inflammatory or tendentious. In contrast, the defense attorney, a partner at a global law firm, refused all comment, which meant that the coverage was going to be totally slanted toward the plaintiff's side.

But that wasn't the worst of it. The defense spokesperson was, by turn, dismissive, obdurate, and self-entitled. He was aghast that the publication was even bothering to cover the case.

When the reporter informed her editor of the defense attorney's bumptious response, she was told to just write what she had, and that he would take a few extra steps of his own. Sensing an opportunity to promote his publication in a national outlet, he sent all the details of the case to *The New York Times*, which expressed keen interest in an email reply. (*Inside Litigation* published a long feature on the Chambers case in its October 1997 edition.)

As the editor now reflects, he would have been less reactive had the defense attorney given some reasonable explanation for his continuing "no comments" to such questions as "Did you check police records to confirm any evidence of prostitution?" and "Is there a movie deal in the works?" In fact, the editor might never have thought to call *The Times*, despite the promotional value, but for the defense attorney's persistent incivility.

The Times never did run the story, but McMath was informed of its interest and he naturally saw no reason to hide it from the opposition. The case may have been weakening on its merits, but the threat of national exposure was one important factor persuading the defense to settle faster and, presumably, for more money.

Certainly, the defense is often constrained from commenting on a case, and the plaintiffs have a natural advantage in the media as a result. But there are ways to level the playing field or, at least, minimize the disadvantage.

McMath was able to win the media skirmish in the Chambers case because—no less than the media advisors counseling the beleaguered hotel franchiser in our previous example—he had an instinctive sense for what was at stake.

That sense extends beyond any single lawsuit. "When you comment in the press, or publish an article in a respected journal, you become part of an ongoing professional dialogue," he says. "You become an opinion-maker. For example, I have published articles on tobacco liability and insurance funds in journals that I knew judges read.

"You must also get the ear of your colleagues on both sides," adds McMath, who has pioneered cases once thought impossible to win, given the media's sturdy First Amendment protection. With a track record of suing newspapers and publishers, McMath has been acutely conscious of just how important it is to maintain friendly relations with the newspapers and publishers he isn't suing.

By appreciating the role of the media, you gain a subtle public imprimatur for your position that is persuasive to friend and foe alike. "What seems like a frivolous case becomes something else entirely when other attorneys see it discussed as a serious substantive matter in a responsible publication," says McMath. Suddenly, summary judgment doesn't seem quite so reliable. On the contrary, a protracted and well-planned media outreach can bring defendants to the settlement table right at the get-go.

EARLY WARNING SIGNS

The hotel owner in our case study above was utterly blindsided by a crisis that he didn't stand much chance of anticipating and planning for. At the same time, crisis managers can take a longer view, foreseeing crises well in advance, if they are instinctively sensitive to the macro-economic and political factors that are breeding grounds for media inquisitions. For example:

What is the industry environment?

Other cases of a crisis nature in your industry are being covered in the media. A reporter in an industry trade publication has started to ask about facts related to what now looks to be a "trend story." Certain industries are more vulnerable to trend stories. Is the industry bleeding, like telecom? The perception is that, as profits go south,everyone is a suspect because everyone is desperate.

Is the industry such a repository of public trust that one betrayal of that trust—by, say, Arthur Andersen—guarantees media interest in other global accounting firms?

Regulatory environment

The Department of Justice or the Securities and Exchange Commission or a member of Congress has indicated they want to watch a particular issue more closely, or political pressure is building to find a whipping boy. Watch every signal their offices send (see Chapter 9). Likewise, monitor state attorneys general in all states where your company has a major presence. State AGs are political animals, and your back may be a good stepladder to power.

Stock performance

For two consecutive quarters, the corporate numbers are down. Coverage of the stock decline is painful enough but reporters will jump at any suggestion that shareholder pressures are forcing inappropriate or illegal responses. At the very least, they will be inspired by the down numbers to sniff around for other negatives. Since you need to prepare a media response that includes positive messages about the stock declines, include as part of that preparation some discussion of what those other negatives might be and how you should respond.

(Continued on page 22)

What's At Stake: Lessons from a Libel Case

Plaintiffs' attorney Sandy McMath had a plan: Get the word out on the libel case he was litigating, get it out now, and get it out responsibly. The defense side had no plan whatsoever, nor any willingness to even play the game. The defense attorney high-handed an obscure newsletter and his client suffered.

The defense case was probably too weak to take to court, although First Amendment defenses can be hard to break. In any event, if you do have to settle a case, effective media planning can at least give you a stronger position at the negotiating table. In its very simplicity, McMath's case offers powerful lessons about the power of the media, and how to survive it:

- No publication is too small not to take seriously. True, if there is a deluge of media requests, you will need to prioritize the publications on your call-back list. But, especially in a day and age when advanced technology can track so much information, any article in any publication can affect your litigation strategy as well as your company's reputation.

- Reasonably explain why you cannot speak on the record. Doing so might suggest that, if you could talk, you'd say something persuasive. In McMath's case, the journalist had no reason to assume the defense side had anything to offer even if the lawyer were empowered to offer it.

- Because you have explained why you can't go public, there's now some trust on the part of the reporter. At that point, go off the record and suggest pointed questions that the reporter might ask the other side. If you can't litigate in the press overtly, you may be able to do so covertly.

- Establish human contact with reporters. Use their first names when you talk to them. Always be polite! Remember Mark Twain's famous warning: Don't pick fights with people who buy ink by the barrel.

(Continued from page 20)

Bad performance news is always reason for any company to go on full media alert.

Stockholder actions

Any action by shareholders legitimizes media interest in every aspect of the company's life. Remember too, lawsuits that name directors and officers often lead to personal interest in the directors and officers themselves. You must anticipate full background checks by reporters. Read the resumes of your directors and officers very carefully. Were any of them ever short sellers? Were any of them ever sued before? How did they get their current jobs, and why? Prepare to defend them as if they were suspects in a crime.

Dangerous practices

Enron got into a lot of trouble with off-balance-sheet assets. Crooked financiers in the 1980s were associated with junk bonds. In fact, off-balance-sheet assets and junk bonds are both perfectly legitimate. But if Enron misuses its instruments, or Ivan Boesky his, you can expect to be called by a suspicious reporter and asked to explain what you're up to if you use them.

Hostile takeovers

As we learned in the 1980s, hostile takeovers open vast frontiers of self-interest. There are a zillion reasons for all sorts of people on both sides of the takeover to say all sorts of things to the media. During a hostile situation, you need to monitor every syllable that gets uttered in public and anticipate those that are about to be uttered.

Non-governmental organizations

You don't need to be the target of a nonprofit organization to go on full alert. Simply be in the industry—as a hedge fund or chemical manufacturer—and you may become the next target. Monitor the

NGO websites and press appearances and think differently about the media if they are targeting the firm or industry next door.

Hot-button issues

Could the obesity cases have been foreseen? Perhaps not, but listen closely for public rumblings that might suggest incipient adversarial interest in your product. For example, many people don't like SUVs. They don't like them for policy reasons ("they guzzle gas"), and they don't like them for political reasons ("people who drive them are suburbanites who don't see the world like us urban animals"). There has already been ample suggestion that SUVs aren't safe either, and we all know where those kinds of suggestions lead.

Past escapes

The Catholic Church incited keen media interest over a decade ago with sexual misconduct charges that soon departed the front page after a leading church official was exonerated. But what could possibly have led to the conclusion that the issue would not someday resurface? Corporations with less painful liabilities should never relax after a brush with scandal or fail to prepare for the media's unwanted return to an unpleasant subject.

Qui tam

What internal dynamics might lead to a public crisis? Have there been widespread layoffs? Is the company known for tough, unreasonable managers? Does employee dissatisfaction hang palpably like a shroud in the home office? Such an environment can foster whistleblowers who will talk to the press, as well as to the government, just a little more readily and a little more enthusiastically, than in a less strained culture.

Faulty products

Pintos do explode. Asbestos does kill. Any genuine product liability matter that crosses the desk of in-house counsel should be treated, for media purposes, as if lawsuits have already been filed and reporter inquiries phoned in. The problem may go away quietly with a responsible corporate initiative. But don't assume it will, and prepare as if it won't.

Not all crises arise or can necessarily be detected from scenarios similar to the above. In fact, some crises come from nowhere. They often involve a hostile reporter who's picked up on something that, from your perspective, is breathtakingly trivial. A permanent media team can hypothesize possible exposures when, for example, a reporter who was hostile to you when he was writing for a local newspaper suddenly gets a job with a national daily.

Remember, media professionals are trained to track not only the news, but the people who report it.

In the next two chapters, we will discuss how to put in place a media team, armed with an effective media plan, sooner rather than later, preferably before a problem arises.

So Don't Forget...

A few fundamental facts underscore just how much is usually at stake when the press trains its focus on your lawsuit...

- The lawsuit itself may be just a small part of what you're up against. First, you must determine what larger agendas drive the litigation. Victory in the press may actually be more important than victory in court.

- Take all publications seriously. A misstep with the editor of a 200-subscriber newsletter can affect coverage in *The New York Times*. Today's information technology is too comprehensive. Don't be cavalier with any reporter.

- Even a minor lawsuit takes on serious dimension if, for whatever reason, a reporter decides to cover it. Suddenly, the garden-variety commercial dispute ostensibly dramatizes an important trend in an industry. Suddenly, the obscure wrongful discharge case ostensibly confirms a long-established pattern of racism.

- Major clients no longer ask that their attorneys be media-savvy, they demand it! As far as they're concerned, the risk to their corporate reputation after litigation is often much greater, in sheer dollars and cents, than the costs and penalties of the lawsuit itself.

THREE

The Quintessential Crisis Team: Two Approaches

One fact is inescapable: Any organization that is likely to find itself on trial in the court of public opinion must have a crisis team in place that includes people able to put a response plan in motion immediately when a crisis arrives.

Most of the major players in high-risk industries have long understood the need for effective crisis teams. For the automobile manufacturers, airlines, big Pharma, alcohol, and, certainly, the tobacco industry, crisis is a fact of life and a cost of doing business. Tires blow, planes crash, pills have side effects, drunks drive, and governments sue. Without a systemic organizational structure in place, these companies would simply not be grappling with the reality of their businesses.

What the crisis team consists of and how it is structured will vary from company to company. Multinational health care corporations are different from banks, banks are different from accounting firms, accounting firms are different from regional construction companies, and so forth.

Within each category, there are also salient differences among organizations. The organization chart at one airline might not look at all like the organization chart at a competitor airline. Some are centralized, and some are decentralized. Reporting relationships might vary from one corporation to another as a result.

(Continued on page 29)

Disparate Examples, Common Lessons

Michelin North America and Andersen show how different organizational structures require different approaches to setting up and managing a crisis team. Michelin is a brand-oriented manufacturer with crisis team members assigned to individual brands. Andersen was a global professional service charged with the delivery of consistent firm-wide messages.

Michelin has never been subjected to withering global scrutiny for alleged malfeasance. Andersen most certainly was.

Because they're so different, the common lessons suggested by the experiences of both organizations are all the more significant. These best practices universally apply in crisis situations, relevant to all types of corporate or professional team formation. For example:

- The crisis team must be in place, with responsibilities clearly delineated, before a crisis occurs.

- An outside PR agency is a good sounding board for ideas and strategies. But, the communications themselves—the actual work of media management during a crisis—must come from the organization's own people. An agency can supply additional arms and legs but ownership of the problem cannot be delegated.

- Technology is always an essential tool. Andersen used a website so its team could unleash a torrent of information. Michelin uses a website to guarantee that the right experts will be assigned to the right crises whenever and wherever they occur.

- It is essential to have lawyers and lobbyists on the crisis team and to encourage open debate among all professional experts. Their instincts are different, and companies must weigh both in the balance in making every important decision during a crisis.

- Arguably, the crisis team should include business-to-business publicists. The skills complement each other. By being close to a particular brand or practice, the publicist can provide valuable information. Also, gaining crisis skills makes publicists better all-around communicators.

- Crisis team members must enjoy the challenge of a crisis or keep out of the way.

(Continued from page 27)

ORGANIZATIONAL FIT

In setting forth crisis team prescriptions, the first variable to consider is size. Some tobacco giants have deemed it necessary to have large permanent teams in place. But, it is impossible for many smaller companies to assume the fixed overhead of an internal team. Even companies with $100 million or more in revenue might be hard pressed to justify such an investment.

However, smaller companies are still not exempt from having to have adequate human resources available. One obvious option is to rely on an outside team at a public relations agency. In some cases, that will entail a monthly retainer or other fee arrangement less onerous than the cost of permanent employees.

Alternatively, smaller companies and organizations can work out arrangements whereby the outside agency creates a crisis team ready to swing into action if called upon to do so. They might bill hourly fees to set up the team and periodically review the company's crisis plan, or to digest new information or developments that will be relevant should a crisis occur.

Among corporations, the crisis teams may need to mirror the organization chart. If a company is decentralized, with numerous and relatively independent business units around the world, those units might need crisis team members knowledgeable on local issues and the local corporate culture. Sometimes, a team member in New

York can adequately master the fact pattern surrounding a crisis in Frankfurt. Other times, that crisis may require language capabilities, knowledge of local law, personal relations with local media and a sense for local public opinion that only someone closer to the situation can provide.

At the same time, some major crises require company-wide co-ordination of effort. No matter how decentralized the organization, it is therefore essential that, in the event of such a crisis, a plan be in effect to bring all the disparate crisis team members into one unified whole, with clearly defined roles and lines of authority.

Another important variable is the law department, since all crisis teams need to include legal counsel. In forming crisis teams, it is necessary to confer with the chief legal officer about which lawyers will be included. Again, some law departments are highly decentralized. Here too, local lawyers might need to be members of local teams but adapt to a company-wide team at a moment's notice.

The structures of some law departments, like General Electric's, are flat. Individual attorneys function almost like partners at a law firm, with their own specific expertise. In these cases, the team formation is easier, as a single lawyer with public affairs experience can be the crisis team's point person.

Two examples of global crisis teams clearly demonstrate how different organizational structures dictate different approaches. Yet in both instances, a similar fundamental objective is achieved: The ready deployment of media-savvy experts able to maximize information flow, handle multiple tasks during a crisis, and deliver a coherent and credible message to the public.

In both cases, the formation of a team and the creation of a crisis plan occur before an actual crisis. Nothing is more essential than to be proactive and set up the structure ahead of time. Once a crisis occurs, there won't likely be time to start interviewing candidates for the job.

BULLET-PROOFING YOUR BRAND

At Michelin North America, Nancy Banks, Director, Public Relations, supervises a team of media professionals with additional personnel available during a crisis. But, a pool of about 50 executives and specialists at various points in the corporation can be immediately added to the team as needed.

Some of these team members are in-house lawyers or C-suite executives. Others are division heads. Others are technical specialists. These team members are the "content experts" who provide the crucial information that the media and the public require in crisis situations.

As a Michelin veteran of over twenty years, Banks knows these 50 people personally and can pick all the adjuncts required for the team as soon as a crisis breaks. Team members can access a proprietary website in the event of a crisis. All potential team members are profiled on the website. If Banks were out of commission, the team formation could thus still go forward. No one would have to worry about identifying the in-house experts or scurry around looking for contact information while the crisis is breaking.

While the website and expert pool guarantee that the right people are assigned to a crisis, the team strategy at Michelin is also determined by which of the several Michelin brands is affected. Banks oversees the Michelin brand in the replacement market and the overall corporate reputation. But, the responsibilities of the two media specialists who report to her are further divided among two other brands: Uniroyal and B.F. Goodrich, as well as the various business units, such as truck tires, cycle tires, etc. "Original equipment" (i.e., the unit that supplies products to vehicle manufacturers) is also treated as a separate division.

Again, organizational structure affects crisis team strategy. A Michelin brand issue might involve corporate and legal as well as product issues. Uniroyal and Goodrich brand issues are usually consumer-oriented. The "Original Equipment" unit is business-to-business, with some direct consumer impact as well. Michelin's strategy assigns responsibility for each to different team members.

Michelin uses an outside PR agency as part of the total crisis team. During a crisis, outside feedback from the agency is often useful as part of the planning process. However, Banks believes that the spokespersons must be from the company itself. It's a matter of credibility, of showing the world that you take the situation seriously enough to handle it yourself.

Once the team is assembled, decisions are made on such crucial questions as, "Do we take a proactive approach and call the media, or do we wait for them to call us?" According to Banks, the answer is always guided by: "What would our customers want us to do?" This priority is good public relations, not just a platitude. For consumer-oriented companies like Michelin, consumers are the final tribunal in any controversy.

Crisis management is a democratic process made possible, says Banks, by a corporate culture that enjoys a significant element of "mutual trust." Early in any crisis, Banks will ask, "Is there anything here we need to be ashamed of?" In this particular corporate culture, she feels she'll get an honest answer.

The decision-making is efficient, albeit democratic, because the team members have been shrewdly selected for their individual expertise. Banks will not question the input of a quality manager who has specific product expertise nor would that manager likely question Banks' assessment of how a particular statement will be greeted by the media.

At the same time, debate between the media experts and legal team members is "healthy." There will always be conflicts between PR professionals and lawyers. The PR instinct is to disclose; the legal instinct is to protect, or to at least be more guarded. Some PR strategies may convince a skeptical public but open the door to a blizzard of litigation, however groundless and unfair it might be. Some legal strategies will exonerate the company in court but alienate the buying public.

Only by allowing for open and sometimes heated debate can the best middle course be determined. In one instance, the legal concerns may be overruled if widespread litigation is finally determined

The 'Holistic' Approach: In-house Counsel as Spokesperson of Choice

Outside counsel often make effective spokespersons during a crisis and some corporate clients, like Steve Hantler at Daimler-Chrysler, even insist that their law firms be prepared to comment on a situation as it unfurls. But, there are dangers. Using outside counsel often gives an appearance that the company has something to hide. Or equally bad, it might seem that the company doesn't take the problem seriously enough to speak for itself.

The Bhopal crisis of the late 1980s is an example of why the choice of spokesperson is so crucial. Faced with liability for the deaths of thousands of Indians, Union Carbide decisively chose a spokesperson from its corporate ranks instead of an effective advocate from the law firm handling the matter, Kelley Drye & Warren.

"This was a legal problem with enormous humanitarian dimensions," says John Callagy, Kelley Drye's chairman. Only by speaking for itself could Union Carbide confirm its profound concern. Yet the choice of spokesperson was also a "holistic" choice, as Callagy puts it. By giving a major media role to Joseph Geoghan, the company's then-general counsel, Union Carbide could be directly responsive to the public, yet manage communications with a sharp eye for potential disclosure liability.In that sense, in-house counsel are indeed a best-of-both-worlds resource; a guardian of strict corporate interest, yet a great deal more than a "legal mouthpiece."

to be an acceptable cost of doing business, and that the highest priority is to convince the world that you are right and ready to prove it in court. Alternatively, the PR concerns may be overruled if there are legal points so important that a protracted public silence is the better part of valor.

IRONIC PARADIGM

If Michelin is a global company that requires different team strategies for different brands, Arthur Andersen was a global organization actuated by a very different concern. With all such professional services firms, the driving need, in or out of crisis, is to confirm a singular global integrity. Generally speaking, at global partnerships (and especially law firms), a partner in Chicago is jointly and severally liable for the behavior of a partner in Caracas. Andersen, with separate partnerships set up in different countries, was something of an exception to that rule. But with Andersen too, clients will still want to be sure that a common ethic ensures consistency everywhere.

Interestingly, we know of no better model for how to set up and manage a crisis team than Andersen's. It is indeed an irony that a firm that endured one of the worst media blitzes in modern history should be such a paradigm, especially as the media campaign implemented by the team ultimately failed to save the day.

Andersen's demise does not belie the soundness of Andersen's media planning or the seaworthiness of its team. The Andersen experience offers a profound caveat to all essays on crisis planning, including our own.

The dismal lesson is that some crises are terminal either because the company is guilty of unforgivable transgressions, or because there are times when no one will believe anything you say, no matter how well directed the media response. It is essential to remember that Andersen's team, set up before the Enron debacle, had always been effective in its handling of media relations for a variety of lawsuits and other institutional skirmishes.

The Andersen crisis team's strategy typifies planning for large partnerships that, however diverse, must fasten on consistent firm-wide messages.

First, set up a crisis committee to be your central planning group as well as the entity from which all other team components can be spun. At organizations like Andersen, the committee typically includes:

- A decision-maker, either the CEO or a senior player reporting to the CEO. This individual must be able to make a determination on all actions and responses at every stage of a crisis, without having to clear it with anyone;

- two or three experienced PR professionals and lobbyists; and

- two or three lawyers.

The immediate purpose of the crisis committee is to articulate the organization's business goals as a guide to all subsequent crisis strategy. Are we trying to save a particular client base? Are we trying to prove that a particular product or service is unaffected by an ongoing crisis? Are we trying to influence the media in a particular geographic region because we plan to open a new office there?

Second, as Chris Hinze, former Worldwide Director of Communications for Andersen Legal, puts it, the crisis committee's function is to "cascade" policy to sub-teams in other affected regions, countries, and cities. Thus, at Andersen, the crisis committee was nationally based in the firm's Chicago headquarters and its Washington, D.C. office. It included staff with expertise in PR, legal, and lobbying. In turn, smaller Andersen teams in London and Hong Kong communicated 24/7 with the worldwide team and with countries in their own time zones to ensure the most consistent message delivery possible.

Third, get your outside media advisors in place and define their roles. At Andersen, outside PR firms were used around the world for three main purposes: To provide independent third-party feedback, to help craft message points, and to deal with the flood of incoming media calls. As at Michelin, the overall policy and day-to-day media contacts were handled by the in-house team.

THE RIGHT STUFF

Such formidable responsibility raises the question: What qualifications should companies look for when staffing crisis teams?

As Hinze observes, the team members must naturally be "calm and objective," and they have to *like* this kind of work. Some PR professionals are great publicists, but they're accustomed to living on the sunny side of the street. They often succeed in getting their companies' business successes noticed, and they know how to get stories published. But they don't necessarily know how to prevent stories from getting published, nor do they recognize that they're in a life-threatening fight where you have to live with bad coverage and still battle to get your messages out.

It's relatively easy to hire battle-tested communications people. You simply ask them if they've ever been involved in a media brouhaha. If so, you call their former bosses and ask how they handled themselves.

Among the professionals who have reported to Banks, one was hired because of PR-agency experience, and the other because of a solid background in community affairs. "Crisis management was not really a consideration when they were hired," says Banks, in part because Michelin has never undergone an ordeal as devastating as the Firestone fracas, much less the Andersen collapse.

In any event, it may not be advisable or practicable to segregate your crisis talent from your promotional or business-to-business staff. Ideally, you want team members capable of handling both sides of the media. "When a major crisis hits, your whole communications staff has to shift into crisis mode and simply forget about doing anything else for the duration," says Hinze.

It's simply less efficient when some business-to-business publicists are able to make the shift, while others still try to conduct business as usual, especially since every journalist in the country just wants to talk about the crisis. Moreover, a talent for handling crisis only makes for better B-to-B. Publicists with a fine-tuned instinct for apprehending problems are able to think faster on their feet, whatever they're selling.

So Don't Forget...

Crisis management is labor-intensive. To manage well, you need a team in place, and you need to apply a number of best practices when you staff that team.

- Set up the team now. Once a crisis occurs, there won't likely be time to start interviewing candidates for the job.

- The team should usually reflect the company's organizational structure. Highly decentralized companies ought to have communications people stationed in different offices. But the overall team structure should allow for efficient decision-making by the team heads, based on input from the far-flung crisis and media managers.

- Include lawyers on the team, and encourage respectful debate between the lawyers and the communications specialists. They bring very different perspectives to the table. Input from both sides is critical if an adequate crisis response is to evolve.

- Pick only team members who enjoy the challenge of this kind of work.

FOUR

The Crisis Plan: From Action Points to Talking Points— and Back to Action

When a crisis arises, the normal response is to either freeze or panic. At corporations, the meltdown can naturally be more spectacular than at smaller companies or with individuals, since many more players are involved. Not knowing what to do, people do nothing, assuming someone else will do it. Even worse, they act, but they act ill-advisedly or at odds with each other.

In such an environment, the media can have a field day. Today, many corporations have crisis plans in place that are activated at the first hint of crisis. A tobacco company or an airline without a crisis plan is unthinkable.

The plan obviously cannot anticipate the specifics of the crisis. But it does provide a framework for going forward coherently. For example, crisis-team formation (discussed in Chapter 3) is inextricably bound up with the crisis plan, simply because the plan usually begins with the necessary steps for assembling the team and assigning responsibilities.

Thus, Michelin's proprietary website is the first place people go when there is a crisis, as all potential team members are profiled there. Director, Public Relations, Nancy Banks, or a surrogate if Banks is unavailable, goes directly to the website and picks the names she'll need. That is Step One in the Michelin crisis plan.

> "There's no such thing as a news cycle anymore, not when online newswires are publishing a story five minutes after something breaks," says Jan Drummond, formerly Sears Roebuck's senior director, external communications.

RATIONAL REACTION

Once a team is assembled in the same room, or via conference call, the media plan provides a template that allows for organized response. Because the crisis plan is created ahead of time, in a calmer environment, it is comprehensive. No vital particulars get lost in the heat of the moment. Thus, questions like, "Should we be proactive with the media or wait for them to call us?" are included as part of the template, guaranteeing that vital point will be covered as early in the crisis as possible.

The plan can list discussion points that dig even deeper. If, for example, the determination is made to be proactive with the media, a follow-up question might be, "Shall we distribute our phone numbers to key press contacts or simply place a few calls?"

At Michelin, the crisis plan itself is posted on the website as an organizational tool for everyone with a need to know. A statement is also posted on the site, usually a simple acknowledgement that a situation has arisen and here is our preliminary response. The statement is adjusted as events develop.

The appropriate people are assigned to gather information about what happened and who was affected. Almost any information can turn out to be important further down the line, so it's veritable detective work that's called for at this point. If a tornado has damaged

(Continued on page 42)

Corporate Crisis Plans Are Sanity Tools

Crisis plans are templates for corporate survival. They provide a structure for a coherent response so that dozens, maybe hundreds, of unofficial spokespersons won't be running around like Chicken Little or, just as bad in some situations, doing nothing and saying nothing. The crisis plan allows a variety of professionals to gather together at once and systematically cover all the bases, methodically plotting their action points and message points.

Michelin's approach typifies at least five advantages of advance planning, without which no corporate crisis plan is complete:

- It utilizes simple technology—a website—to organize the agenda.

- The plan itself allows for the formation of an organized team drawn from the ranks of the entire company.

- It allows for thorough information-gathering.

- It provides a preliminary media response and forces the crisis team to strategize a specific media plan sooner rather than later.

- It forces the crisis team to articulate questions to which they don't yet have answers but will need sooner rather than later.

The very existence of a crisis plan creates an immediate awareness in the corporate ranks that some response is needed or that a decision to not respond at least be a conscious and strategic decision. It's all about "ensuring that management understands that bad news doesn't age well," says Nancy Banks, Michelin's Director, Public Relations.

The ideal crisis plan is one that takes on a life of its own, mobilizing people for responsible action simply because there's a plan in force that calls on them to take that action.

(Continued from page 40)

a plant, how was the rest of the community affected? What are other companies experiencing? Following the crisis plan, certain team members will check the effects on inventory—how many tires were destroyed, ancillary damage to the plant, etc.

Following the crisis plan, the media team is brought in at a point where the preliminary information-gathering by the company is already underway and the news of the crisis has circulated. It's at this point that the question of being proactive with the media arises. Preliminary message points are also drawn up. They will be expanded or refined as events unfurl.

The next step in the crisis plan calls for action by Michelin personnel, specifically on two fronts: Whom do we need to help? Whom do we need to contact?

The tornado example is a pointed one, as a Michelin plant in Fort Wayne, Indiana, was damaged by a severe storm a few years ago. "Whom to help" obviously encompasses employees and their families or other members of the community that the company can assist. "Whom to contact" would include government officials and possibly other businesses in the community, as well as the media.

Again, as these actions are set in motion in accordance with the plan, the earlier tasks usually need to be revisited. More information will need to be incorporated on the website, and the message points or the media crisis plan itself might change.

The next item on the crisis plan is: What don't we know at this point that we need to know? And, how do we find it out? If a severe storm hits Fort Wayne, a main question to answer at this point is, "Will the plant be inoperative and for how long?"

By now, we're no longer dealing with a natural disaster or common enemy. Suddenly, there's a PR liability as well, since the community will want to know if people will lose their jobs, or if Michelin even intends to repair or replace the facility. (After the Fort Wayne tornado, repairs were made quickly, no jobs were lost, and there were no injuries to workers.)

The crisis plan thus allows for a neat transition from administrative disaster planning to a potentially more delicate media planning; in other words, from action points to talking points.

FIFTEEN MILLION HOUSE CALLS

It's not just high-risk industries such as air transportation or tobacco that are particularly attuned to the need to have a crisis plan in place. Any major retailer should know that, in the event of a crisis, a massive corporate stonewall will likely alienate customers and jeopardize revenue worldwide.

Sears, Roebuck and Co. is a major retailer.

The company knows that bad press of any sort isn't only about reputation. It's about money. In 2002, for instance, Sears had more than 25 million active credit customers. Over the years, the company's diversified holdings have included real estate development units like Homart (divested in the mid-1990s) as well as financial services.

Sears employees make 15 million house calls to customers every year. Trouble can thus come from anywhere, and the effects of real trouble could be inestimable. That being the case, it's surprising that, as Jan Drummond, Sears' former Senior Director, External Communications, confirms, the company did not have a formal crisis plan in place until 2000.

The reason may reflect one of the important points we made in Chapter 3: Media management requires the enthusiastic and responsive participation of the in-house legal team.

When Sears finally did write a formal crisis plan, the timing coincided with the in-house rise of then-General Counsel Anastasia Kelly, who by all accounts is an unusually gifted legal manager with a keen eye for how different parts of the corporate picture must fit together. There's a lot more to running a law department than the law.

(Continued on page 46)

Issues Management...A Definition

Manly Molpus has a two-part definition of "issues management." The first part suggests why issues management often fails. The second part identifies the consequences of failure.

"Issues management is a thoughtful analysis of a potentially critical issue, with an action plan by which a point of view can be effectively advocated," says Molpus, principal of The Molpus Advisory Group, LLC and former President and CEO of the Grocery Manufacturers Association.

"Effective issues management avoids government regulation and brand damage," adds Molpus.

Beneath its straightforward surface, Molpus' definition really tells us why most issues campaigns are stillborn, assuming they're ever conceived in the first place. In order to render a "thoughtful analysis of...potential problems," a corporation must look beyond simple PR plans that merely lay out practicable talking points for responding to future challenges.

On the one hand, issues management also requires assessment of the public's attitudinal proclivities and how a situation or debate will likely play out in light of dominant public values. Such assessment underscores the advantages and disadvantages that a company, industry, or institution will encounter once an issue finally bubbles up into a national controversy.

During Molpus' years in the food industry, for example, childhood obesity was a litigious issue. Instinctively, at least, food industry advocates understood that plaintiffs' attempts to blame restaurants would confront a deeply abiding public value—that what children eat or don't eat is the responsibility of their parents, not the CEO of McDonald's or Burger King. A deeply rooted antagonism to this potentially burgeoning species of litigation was thus an asset for the industry from the get-go.

On the other hand, most companies fail at issues management because it requires an investment in monitoring issues long before they become crises or lawsuits. That kind of advance action—often 10 years in advance—runs against the grain of corporate behavior, which is typically reactive to whatever problems have already materialized in the form of bad press, ominous elections, or hostile investigations.

As such, the challenge for communications professionals is to sell a need-to-have strategy that C-Suites, burdened by more immediate disputes and imbroglios, typically perceive as a nice-to-have strategy. Maybe the best way to do so is by showing those C-Suites the benefits of past issues management—and by conclusively demonstrating how a model proactive campaign came into being and finally served the vital interests of its sponsors.

One such example was the early effort of the food and drug industries to defeat a grassroots movement to label foods containing genetically modified organisms (GMO). If U.S. companies were well ahead of the curve on this issue, it's no doubt because companies in Europe and elsewhere in the world were so far behind it. U.S. companies could not escape the evidence: Because so little spade work had been done overseas, there are now 19 countries that require GMO labeling.

In 2002, the GMO issue came to a ballot in Oregon where 80% of voters initially favored labeling. Because the industry had prepared itself well in advance of that election—with polling, with focus groups, with creative enlistment of third-party supporters—the numbers were reversed and the referendum defeated.

Particularly heartening to the industry, the victory came in Oregon—possibly the state most likely to support GMO labeling.

Which brings us to the second half of Molpus' definition. If industry does not manage issues well in advance, a void is created that government regulators invariably fill. Those regulators are directly responsive to what they perceive to be the will of the people. If you don't bend that will over time, others will.

(Continued from page 43)

Drummond believes that the success she had in both creating and implementing a crisis plan is directly attributable to the fact that any of her team members could consult with any member of the law department at any time. "Sometimes we [needed] an immediate answer to a question," says Drummond. "Our communications staff members [knew] they [could] interrupt the lawyers during a meeting or grab them in the hall."

The crisis plan grew out of a series of brown-bag lunches that Drummond held with what would become known as her "Critical Incident Communications" team. They developed a worksheet based on a series of What Ifs: What if the company is involved in a hostile takeover? What if a plane crashes into one of the stores?

Specific follow-ups were posed. How much media coverage would one situation generate versus another? Are there opportunities amid the crisis to get out positive messages about the company, and how should those be expressed in the context of a tragedy or a scandal?

The document that evolved from these meetings, called the Critical Incident Communication worksheet, became the de facto Sears crisis plan. By hypothesizing the media dimensions of certain kinds of crises, and investing considerable time in the process, Drummond and her team began to define audiences—the relatives of victims, civic leaders, customers, shareholders, etc.—and articulate possible responses to a variety of critical situations.

Sears has gone beyond most companies in that the communications team developed, not just a template, but usable content that might be applied in future crisis situations.

As at most companies that have effective crisis plans in place, the document is shared with selected representatives from departments that might be involved in the situation and possibly included on a crisis team: the chairman, human resources, legal, finance, individual business units, and the corporate ethics group.

For a crisis of any magnitude, a core crisis group (including the CEO, general counsel, and the senior vice president of public relations and communications) begins immediately to formulate the crisis response. Representatives from the rest of the company are appointed as needed; in some circumstances, the active team can include dozens of individuals from various segments of the company. The members of Sears' "external communications" staff included a Director of Corporate Reputation and a financial media relations expert as well as Drummond.

The crisis plan template enumerates a fundamental step-by-step process, including:

- Team development, based on the specific expertise of individuals throughout the company;

- assignment of responsibilities and tasks;

- information development and information flow among team members during the course of a crisis; and

- defining all audiences and articulating special issues or problems related to each audience.

This last step takes us well beyond process and into content and messages. For a company like Sears that depends on the general public for its livelihood, message development can be a gargantuan, but delicate task.

Recently, for example, Sears decided to extend employee benefits to same-sex couples. Since it has a conservative customer base, this decision could have precipitated a crisis. But, the communication team was able to prepare appropriate message points in advance, which allowed Sears to support its policy without alienating its friends.

Not all potential crises become actual crises. The additional value of a well-wrought crisis plan is its flexibility. It can be useful to prepare for possible problems as well as real ones. Similarly, some problems develop slowly and the media crisis plan can be worked over in anticipation of an expected media barrage.

The crisis plan emphasizes speed: Getting the journalist to the right spokesperson fast. "There's no such thing as a news cycle anymore," says Drummond, "not when online newswires are publishing a story five minutes after something breaks."

Not being available for comment is unacceptable. A wire service will publish whatever information it has and report that the company's spokesperson could not be reached for comment. Newspapers throughout the country then pick up that report. As they reprint the wire information, they're still saying, even a week later, that the company's representative could not be reached for comment.

Staffing is one area where Drummond sounds a different note than what we heard in Chapter 3 from Nancy Banks and Chris Hinze. For companies like theirs, media crisis experience is certainly a plus, but Drummond wants media team members who have definitely "been through the wringer."

"They must know how the media works, and they must understand what the media wants," says Drummond. They must also know when the news is going to be bad, and why you sometimes just have to swallow unfair coverage.

During the Enron scandal, for example, a reporter called with questions about Sears' off-balance-sheet assets. There is nothing wrong with companies like Sears having assets off the balance sheet, but, in the Enron environment, it was Drummond's job to manage expectations among Sears employees. Some uninformed and negative mention in the press was likely.

Such crucial internal communication doesn't happen naturally or serendipitously. It happens because there is an internal structure that allows and encourages interaction during a crisis. Again, crisis team formation and crisis plans are inseparable. The plans bring the teams into existence and the team members breathe life into the plans.

THE SEARS CRISIS PLAN IN ACTION

Two things set Sears, Roebuck and Co. apart from most companies: One, a crisis plan has existed since 2000 that allows for immediate planning on all important fronts, including media communications. Two, Sears' in-house lawyers have an acute sense of the importance of PR and take their role in the development of a crisis response very seriously.

As a result, Sears has superior resources for incorporating input from its media communications team into a case strategy. A lawsuit the company filed against Emerson Electric provides a perfect example.

Emerson is a Sears supplier, so Sears felt the need to tread carefully in how it handled the media dimension of the litigation. On the other hand, Sears suspected what Jan Drummond, until recently Sears' Senior Director, External Communications, describes as "active fraud" on the part of some Emerson employees.

A law department/PR department meeting focused on whether to proactively contact the press with Sears' side of the story. A working statement to the press was vetted by both departments and Emerson's likely reactions to the statement were measured. The "business decision" was to go public proactively, as a message to Emerson that Sears was very serious about this litigation.

The combined wisdom of the legal and PR experts resulted in a compromise strategy that would put Emerson on notice, but not put Emerson in a position where it would have to lash back with all it had. This solution, says Drummond, was to call the press but "not flog the story for a week or two." She would just deliver Sears' message and then back off for a bit.

In lieu of a press release, Drummond left voice mails—it was a Friday afternoon—with her contacts at *Reuters,* the *Associated Press,* and a couple of newspapers. It was a fairly big story for a few days but then, as planned, it faded into oblivion. Sears made its point, but Emerson was left with wiggle room.

The key words: "as planned." It was an articulate strategy made possible because a crisis plan existed that put company lawyers into the same room with company PR pros at a crucial juncture in the evolving story.

So Don't Forget...

The crisis plan is your crisis team's indispensable blueprint. It sets forth basic policies and procedures. It also allows for enough flexibility so that team members can adopt specific action points in response to specific problems. It lists the essential questions that need to be asked at the outset of any crisis. Among the plan's key elements:

- It is proactive, drawn up before a crisis. Because it is written during the calm before a storm, significant points —questions like "Should we call the media or wait for the media to call us?"—are less likely to be omitted.

- It directs team members to define all information that will be needed and how that information can be gathered. It also focuses team members on information not yet available and on where such information might be obtained.

- It assigns specific roles and responsibilities to each team member.

- It defines the vital audiences: consumers, family members of disaster victims, shareholders, etc.

- It is available, often on a website, to all need-to-know crisis team members, 24/7.

FIVE

Handling the Print Interview

There are primarily three types of media that you may expect to encounter during a crisis: print, broadcast (TV and radio), and Internet (blogs, in particular). In this chapter, we'll take a look at the print media.

MESSAGE POINTS

The first step is to work with your media team to craft "message points."

"Where there is, or likely to be, substantial media coverage, a primer of stock phrases is not useful," says James Eiszner, head of the antitrust group at Shook, Hardy & Bacon in Kansas City, Missouri. "Careful, early work with the client and, ideally, a media specialist, is important to develop a few themes that are solidly supported and to brief spokespersons on how those themes should be delivered to the media."

These messages are the points that you must get across in no uncertain terms. They are the distilled essence of what you want to say to the world and what you want the world to believe. They communicate your key position on all the basic issues confronting you or your business in the current crisis.

Likewise important, message points keep you focused. They help you avoid volunteering distracting information that is irrelevant to your position or to what you want to get across—distracting information that could supplant your real message points when the reporter sits down to write the story. If you don't stay on point, your digression may be the only quote from you that appears in the story.

Ideally, your message points will dominate and influence the perception of the interviewer both during the interview and afterward. At the very least, they will be credible enough to make it more difficult for reporters to publish negative facts and opinions about you without feeling the need to add some balance or equivocation.

Practice your message points continually until you are able to enunciate them without sounding as if they're memorized. The more a part of your consciousness these message points become, the better you'll be able to use them to buttress your response to a broad array of questions.

Note the sidebar on page 54 with sample message points related to one of the most notorious media crises in recent history—the Catholic Church sex scandals. Consider two things about them.

First, they're relatively brief. True, you may need to elaborate on additional details during an interview. But you should always return to your message points; i.e., "bridge" back to them, as we discuss below. In all interviews, don't forget how important it is to repeat message points. By going back to them, you virtually force reporters to include in their coverage what you believe are the most important points.

Second, they are matter-of-fact, simple and declarative as possible. You do not want to be argumentative or defensive or exhortatory. The key is to stay on track, not to be carried away by your own emotion or conviction.

You will want to confer with your media team to determine the tone with which you deliver the message points. "Matter-of-fact" should not mean bland. Some message points ought to be delivered, if not argumentatively, then passionately.

> "We all recognize that many [business] situations are not black and white," comments Rick Schmitt, a staff writer for *The Los Angeles Times*. "There are always shades of gray" that can be used to balance the story.

Imagine a businesswoman who, after three decades of unimpeachable professional integrity, is suddenly and unjustly accused of stealing. To be effective, the message point refuting the charge should be delivered with the simple conviction, dignity, and power that anyone would expect of someone in this position.

This businesswoman can underscore basic declarative points with restrained but palpable emotion. For example: "Not once in thirty years has anyone accused me of impropriety. Not once has anyone brought such allegations to my attention privately. Suddenly, I am being publicly accused of impropriety. I am profoundly disappointed that someone would choose to make these allegations in this manner."

The content of the message point includes two forceful elements: past innocence, and the odd fact that no one brought the situation to her attention except in a sudden, public context. It thus shifts the moral burden back onto the shoulders of the accuser.

There is also clear room for strategic emotion. Reporters are usually human and they're impressed by passion if it is measured and intelligent. Note that the repetition of the phrase "Not once" allows for emphasis in the delivery. It is a rhetorical device that communicates logic combined with righteous force.

You may need to craft message points that acknowledge a painful truth that you simply cannot talk around. Especially in a business context that does not involve malfeasance but does involve a

(Continued on page 55)

Sample Message Points: A Church under Siege

No media-feeding in recent years has been more frenzied than the response to the sex scandals endured by the Catholic Church. Here is a sample of the kind of effective messaging that was used successfully at one point and would have likewise well-served all affected Archdioceses and Orders.

1. Our hearts go out to all victims of sexual abuse, and we are fully available to anyone who has been victimized. We will cooperate fully with civil authorities as they undertake their investigations, and we will impose all appropriate punitive measures on our end.

2. If individuals are found to have been innocent, it is our hope that you will join us in exonerating these people as zealously and as persistently as they have been accused and investigated.

3. Because allegations of misdoing are now so rife and highly publicized, we must be doubly vigilant to protect innocent clergy who may be accused, especially as, in this atmosphere, disturbed individuals, or malevolent individuals, may see an opportunity to lodge false but damaging allegations.

Notice that the message points above do not include an expression of confidence that the investigation will fully vindicate the accused. In fact, attorneys counsel against that message.

"The most helpful comment is that your client is 'cooperating fully with the investigation,'" advises William Sampson, a partner in the Overland Park, Kansas, office of Shook, Hardy & Bacon. By contrast, "expressing confidence that the investigation will vindicate the client may antagonize the prosecutor, who will then be less inclined to negotiate with you if the investigation does turn up something," according to Sampson, who defends white-collar criminal as well as civil cases.

(Continued from page 53)

serious economic setback, be straight with the journalist. At the same time, develop message points that can ameliorate the perception of crisis or even suggest positive dimensions.

"We all recognize that many [business] situations are not black and white," comments Rick Schmitt, a staff writer for *The Los Angeles Times*. "There are always shades of gray" that can be used to balance the story.

Let's say four partners have just left your accounting firm and taken $10 million in business to a competitor. "Maybe it's just as well they left," says Schmitt. "Maybe they have a history of jumping firms."

It's quite possible the other firms they left have prospered in the intervening years. Or, adds Schmitt, maybe there were cultural incompatibilities that actually reflect well on your firm if, for instance, your firm is a very collegial, cooperative place, and the departing partners are 900-pound gorillas who must have everything their way all the time.

Don't deny the $10 million loss or pretend it won't sting. But emphasize in your message points a persistent reason why the reporter and his or her readers will be sympathetic and even want to root for you in the months ahead.

As Schmitt agrees, these ameliorating factors, these "shades of gray," may wind up taking up more space in the article than the specific adverse event.

Finally, no matter how bad the crisis, there may always be an opportunity to deal with it in a way that accentuates a positive, so much so, perhaps, that the ultimate effect of the media crisis is to enhance your reputation to an extent where it's even stronger than before the crisis began.

A single strategic message point may sometimes accomplish this happy reversal. In the late 1990s, a partner at a major law firm had

(Continued on page 57)

Sample Q&A: Setting the Agenda Yourself

Here's how the Catholic Church might have "bridged" to simple and eloquent message points, despite unpredictable questions designed to lure the interviewees into perilous extraneous comment.

Q: *Tell me something, why do so many priests get in trouble?*

A: As a non-Catholic sociologist at Penn State, Phillip Jenkins, has documented, sexual abuse is no more common among priests than among any other group in society. Clearly, though, we need to be more open to discussing the pressures and temptations they face on a day-to-day basis, even as we need to have a zero-tolerance policy for priests who give in to the worst of those temptations. If individuals are found to have been innocent, it is our hope that you will join us in exonerating these people as zealously and as persistently as they have been accused and investigated.

Q: *What of the allegation that accused priest John Doe has a "split personality?"*

A: We don't engage in speculation about what's in others' minds, and we expect the same in return. If we uncover misdeeds, we will take all appropriate punitive measures, including summary dismissal from the Order. We have only known Father Doe to be an inspiring, loving, demanding, and respectful pastor. Just as it is difficult to imagine the pain of sexual abuse, so too is it difficult to imagine the horror of being wrongfully accused of such a misdeed.

Q: *What about all the dossiers that our sources say they sent to the Vatican, and which never once generated a response?*

A: No one has ever seen these dossiers except the people who allegedly wrote them. We don't know what's in them; we don't even know they really exist. You can't condemn a human being on the basis of secret dossiers that no one's seen. That's Orwellian. That offends common decency. If individuals are found to have been innocent, it is our hope that you will join us in exonerating these people as zealously and as persistently as they have been accused and investigated. Just as it is difficult to imagine the pain of sexual abuse, so too is it difficult to imagine the horror of being wrongfully accused of such a misdeed.

(Continued from page 55)

stolen millions and was able to get away with it because his particular practice was so esoteric that no one detected the thievery.

The firm's message point was this: "As most major law firms continue to grow and add on abstruse specialties, it becomes harder for anyone to feel totally safe." The second part of the message point was the coup de grace that deflected the whole issue well beyond the firm itself, even as it underscored the essential integrity of the firm. Message: "If it can happen here, it can happen anywhere." (See Chapter 13 for more on this salient law firm media success.)

BRIDGING OVER TROUBLED WATERS

Watch the world's successful politicians. No matter what reporters ask them, they always find a way to conclude their answers by repeating whatever point is in their interest to make.

"Senator, do you deny that you stole $25,000?"

"I do deny it, and I am sure that the special prosecutor's report will vindicate me so that I can get back to the job that the people of my great state elected me to do—which is to reduce taxes. It is so important that we get a fair tax and that we not burden America's businesses and entrepreneurs with bloated government spending."

"Senator, are you worried about Suzie Johnson testifying that she saw you steal the money?"

"The special prosecutor will evaluate all testimony for what it's worth, assuming it's worth anything. I have full faith in the special prosecutor and that the justice system will take its course so that we can return to the real business of the United States Senate, which is to reduce taxes. It is so important that we get a fair tax and..."

In a corporate or personal crisis, it is essential to direct the flow of dialogue as much as possible. Our senator quoted above may be a disingenuous rascal, but his technique is sound. Bridge back to your message points at all times. At best, it will get the reporter off some nagging detail that will distract him or her from the essential message that you want to get across. At the least, it will provide one more opportunity for you to remind the reporter what the message is.

Bridging thus allows you to influence the main theme of an article that is being written about you, rather than waiting around to see which ancillary detail—a detail that may be damaging, and is certainly not important to your purposes in any event—the reporter chooses to spotlight. Along with your message points, work with your media team on a hypothetical Q&A that incorporates the messages and constantly bridges back to them.

Message points are the heart and soul of how to communicate with the media during a crisis. Hang them on the wall where you can clearly see them while you're talking on the phone.

At the same time, there are a number of necessary best practices that should hang right alongside the message points. They are rules to live by in a crisis.

Brevity is the soul of wit

Don't be afraid to keep your mouth shut after you make your point to a reporter. One inveterate trick that sly reporters use, especially in a phone interview, is to say nothing after you finish talking. A full

30 seconds might go by before they get to their next question. Their scheme is to make you feel uncomfortable enough to nervously blurt out something you shouldn't say.

Disclose all (usually)

Yes, be brief in your responses, but comprehensive in covering the bases. Don't let the reporters find out something for themselves. Take a cue from prosecutors who during a trial will reveal a plea bargain before the defense side has a chance to do so. Reporters will likely find out what you don't want them to know anyway, and then come back and confront you with the information, loaded for bear. By telling them yourself, you minimize the impact of the information.

No "no comments"

Pre-Enron studies showed that 62 percent of Americans equated "no comment" with "we're guilty." The numbers have only gone up since Enron. "No comment" concedes the entire story to the opposing point of view and possibly even communicates indifference.

"Many executives and a lot of lawyers share the same personality disadvantage, and that is the need to maintain absolute control," observes litigator Howard Scher, a partner in the Philadelphia office of Buchanan Ingersoll & Rooney. "We have customarily equated absolute control with saying 'no comment' whenever confronted by the media.

"It is a dangerously unsophisticated way to deal with a media inquiry," adds Scher. "We can and should provide information that won't come back to haunt us if we're careful about it. We can also learn something about our own cases—both how the public (and potential jurors) perceive it, and what our opponents are thinking—by engaging in an ongoing dialogue with the media. 'No comment' actually means less, not more control."

(Continued on page 61)

Message Point Support: Harnessing a Groundswell of Goodwill

Among the best practices for developing and delivering message points, you may sometimes find a most effective weapon at your disposal, even in situations doused in controversy. It's called third-party endorsement, a thunderous affirmation of your point and of your company's credibility by an outside party that may be so powerful as to sweep all press coverage in your direction.

Here is an example: When litigator Christopher Caldwell and his firm, Los Angeles' Caldwell, Leslie, Newcombe & Pettit, began representing Dr. Paul Fleiss, father of accused Hollywood madam Heidi Fleiss, it was "late in the game," as Caldwell recalls. Charges of falsely cosigning a home loan for his daughter had already been filed against the prominent pediatrician. (He stipulated that he would be occupying the house, which was not the case.) It was an "outrageous" attempt by the prosecutor to use Dr. Fleiss to pressure Ms. Fleiss into a plea bargain, according to Caldwell.

Dr. Fleiss eventually pled out and kept his license. And the judge publicly questioned the prosecutor's tactics. That questioning was duly noted in the press. Yet the caliente nature of the story was such that media mismanagement might have still wounded Dr. Fleiss' reputation and caused immense personal pain.

Fortunately, that reputation was the best resource for Caldwell. Fleiss was a veritable "saint," a doctor who tended to the poor, and from some of those patients "took vegetables for payment" in lieu of money, as Caldwell puts it. Over 700 letters in praise of Dr. Fleiss were gathered. Approximately 200 mothers and children turned up in court. Remember *Miracle on 34th Street*?

Yet, Caldwell took no chances. He personally talked with every reporter before he let his client do so, and then rehearsed Dr. Fleiss to ensure he would not say anything wrong. A powerful two-part message point evolved: (1) here was a selfless community servant who (2) only did for his daughter what most any father would have done. When the judge also repeated the second part of the message in open court, it was game, set, and match as far as the media was concerned.

While Caldwell was wise in his circumspection, the client did enjoy an additional, rather unusual advantage. Some reporters at *The Los Angeles Times* were parents, and their pediatrician of choice was Paul Fleiss. Nothing like a third-party endorsement from the reporter down the hall!

(Continued from page 59)

Paint when you talk

All the great communicators win their points by making them in a way that people can see. Remember the hanging chads in the Florida 2000 Presidential election…those visible entities told a story that made the opposition look ridiculous. On the other hand, there was no equally vivid picture in the Democratic complaint that African-Americans were being disenfranchised. As a result, George W. Bush became President of the United States.

Be human

Small things go a long way. For instance, use the reporter's first name during the interview. Establishing personal contact lessens the chance the reporter will take a cheap shot or publish something negative that isn't absolutely substantiated.

Know the rules

During a crisis, it is especially important to know the difference between "on the record," "off the record," and "not for attribution." Off the record means the reporters cannot print what you say in any context (although they can print it if the information is obtained through other sources or becomes public). Not for attribution means they can print it, but not name you in the process. Rare is the

journalist who doesn't honor the agreement but you must clearly set
the rule before you answer a single question.

Know about the reporter

Is the journalist an investigative reporter by trade? Has he or she
been tough or unfair in the past? There may not be a lot of time for
a background check, but get what you can. If the reporter is a pit
bull, you will have to face the grilling, but, the more you know, the
more you will be able to gear your comments to the reporter's level
of sophistication.

There are even subtle ways to make a journalist a little more
modest and affect the coverage to your advantage. Let's say you run
a computer company and you're being sued for patent infringement. If you dwell on the complexity of the technical material, even
sophisticated reporters may be daunted and less confident about
jumping to conclusions than if they were covering a sex scandal.

Play for time

Researching the background of the reporter requires time, so don't
respond to interviews just when the reporters call. Find out their
deadline, and promise to get back to them early enough. Then use
that breathing space to research the reporter and, if necessary, the
newspaper or magazine itself. It also allows time to further rehearse
or modify your message points. Always get back to them before
their deadline, even if just to say that you cannot comment on this
particular issue at this moment. At least you've shown a professional
courtesy that will likely be appreciated.

Many of the points we've made in this chapter are equally sound
whether the media involved is a newspaper or a prime-time television broadcast. But the dynamics can also be fundamentally different, depending on whether you're being interviewed by Ben Bradlee
or Ed Bradley.

That brings us to the subject of our next chapter, which is
knowing the difference between print and broadcast media expectations and how, in a crisis, you need to prep differently for both.

So Don't Forget...

Once the planning and staffing of the crisis plan is completed, implementation begins. At the heart of implementation is the press interview itself. To maximize positive press coverage:

- Have succinct message points in place. These are simple, declarative statements that summarize your "case." Write them down. During phone interviews, have them in front of you.

- Repeat the message points at every possible point during the interview. "Bridge" back to them as often as possible. Don't worry that reporters may sense your reliance on this tried-and-true tactic. Repetition will still maximize the likelihood that you will be quoted in your own carefully crafted language.

- Matter-of-fact doesn't mean bland. Even the most carefully worded message point can be delivered with passion and conviction.

- Devise hypothetical Q&As to guide you during the interview. Include negative questions and come up with practicable responses.

- Work toward a relationship with reporters. A good relationship increases the chances of good coverage. Little things, like calling reporters by their first names, go a long way.

How to Survive the Broadcast Media Pit Bulls

All of the dangers encountered when dealing with the print media are magnified tenfold when the television cameras are rolling.

The impact of a mistake is obviously greater because the audience is so vast. A mistake can also be replayed on the air all day long or longer if it's important or juicy enough. How many times have you seen President Clinton wag his finger in denial of sexual misconduct? Dozens of times? Hundreds?

The stakes are therefore enormous. In many instances, what happens during those three or four visual bites that run on the evening news can be a great deal more decisive for your company and perhaps for you personally than anything that happens in the courtroom.

The chances that you will be misrepresented are also greater. The television interview process does not permit the give-and-take that allows reporters to conscientiously approximate the truth in a fair news venue. There are no six-paragraph appendages qualifying the point of the story with caveats and counter-claims. There is just the raw, naked point itself. You have ten seconds to make it. Your adversary gets ten seconds too.

(Continued on page 68)

Hi, This Is Fox News. Can We Talk to You For A Minute?

There was quite a surprise waiting for the founder of a government contracting firm at the forefront of controversies over private interests supporting American war efforts in Iraq.

As the gentleman left his suburban home in the morning, a camera crew from a national television network was waiting for him, eager to discuss a lawsuit charging that his company was culpable in the ghastly murders of their workers.

The term of art is "ambush interview." The target's response was not atypical. He simply refused to talk and then jumped as fast as possible into his SUV. The cameras kept rolling—and the CEO looked very much like a man in hiding.

The bad news is that hardly anyone in a position of authority is exempt from the ambush interview. (The few exceptions include high-ranking government officials with 24/7 Secret Service protection.) The good news is that there are skill sets any corporate spokesperson can develop to survive the experience.

Ambush interviews may be unforeseen, but they are not unforeseeable. Companies proactive enough to prepare for crises, before crises arise, are also typically proactive enough to train their key executives in the fine art of handling media inquiries—both what to say, and how to say it. There's every reason in today's world to include the ambush interview on the training curriculum.

With ambush interviews, the *how* is always all about minimizing the peril of the immediate situation in which you've been taken by surprise and may say the absolute worst thing. The best response is to politely try and set another time and place for the interview. There's often little or no chance the reporter will agree to do so, since it would defeat the purpose of his or her trying to ambush you in the first place. But it's worth a shot, and the best way to take that shot is by politely asking the reporter what the deadline is.

If you're able to schedule an alternative time that fits comfortably within the deadline, it becomes more difficult for the reporter to refuse your reasonable request. Take any reprieve granted you to prepare and test yourself. Clear your head, gain your composure, and *always* consult at once with someone else —a communications advisor, ideally—about what to say when the interview resumes. Even talking to your Aunt Mae is better than nothing as it at least provides a different perspective.

If the reporter absolutely refuses an alternative schedule, some sort of response is still preferable to "no comment." That response should include only one or two central message points expressed as briefly as possible. Say nothing but what you want used on air or in print, and, if the reporter presses you further, conclude with "That's all the comment I have at this point."

By deciding *now* what those central messages will be *then*, you arm yourself with permanent ready-made alternatives to "no comment." Develop messages that tailor your response to a variety of bad-case scenarios (e.g., a product recall has happened, the product has killed someone, the FDA is investigating the product, etc.)

The same delivery skills applicable to all broadcast interviews are applicable to ambushes—only more so. For example:

- Look directly at the camera or the interviewer. If you don't, you'll look guilty no matter what you say, especially when the audience knows you were caught by surprise. One darkish downward glance can become the dominant image.

- Speak in sound bites. The less explanation, the better. The less verbiage, the better. Don't give the editor a lot of choice about what to cut and what to broadcast.

- In any interview, it's always important to not repeat a negative but at no time is it more important than during an ambush interview. You don't want the entire broadcast to be nothing more than your assertion that "I didn't do it."

(Continued from page 65)

For attorneys, who make their living exercising control, it's the most challenging media experience imaginable because here they have no control. They can't ask to verify direct quotes prior to a broadcast as they can with the print media. Worst of all, TV coverage is ruled by film editors who can and usually do whittle your comments down to whatever they want to run and in whatever context they want to run it. The most astute commentary can look ludicrously fatuous once it finally airs.

Alas, it's very difficult to decline a TV appearance, especially in a high-profile case when the cameramen and reporters simply show up and stick the microphone in your face. In such situations, accused criminals bury their faces in drawn-up overcoats. For the rest of us, that's not an option.

"In Illinois, the cameras are not allowed in the courtroom," says Kimball Anderson, a partner at Winston & Strawn in Chicago. "But the reporters will greet you in the hallway of the court building— and they're very good at blocking the exits!"

You may also have to go on TV because your opponent is doing so. It's a defensive measure that, if it doesn't help your company, at least minimizes the harm that television coverage inevitably causes. With TV, damage control is often the best you can hope for as you answer charges by a prosecutor or opposing counsel, perhaps, or defuse rampant media speculation and fervid public gossip.

On the other hand, TV is not without its potential for concrete positive gains. Richard Ben-Veniste, a partner in the Washington, D.C. office of Mayer, Brown, Rowe & Maw, believes that, if you maintain a "reasoned, temperate" demeanor in front of the camera, "avoiding bombast," you can quiet "some of the hype and frenzy," some of the Chicken Little hubbub that may surround the case, especially if the "media pack has been headed in the other direction" against you.

Ben-Veniste is a veteran of many on-air encounters with angle-hungry TV reporters. During the 1970s, he was the 29-year-old Chief of the Watergate Special Prosecutor's Office for the Department of Justice. A decade later, he represented lawyer Howard Criden, accused of setting up the payoffs in the ABSCAM scandal. A decade after that, he was minority counsel to the U.S. Senate in the Whitewater investigation.

THE BEST WAYS TO SAY NOTHING

Kimball Anderson warns that any commentary to reporters outside the courtroom opens both lawyer and client to defamation charges.

"You cannot repeat allegations," says Anderson, a partner at Winston & Strawn who represented the estate of Suzanne Olds, bludgeoned to death after a nasty divorce from her husband, Dean Olds.

Mr. Olds, one of the leading intellectual property attorneys in the country, had taken up with a young German male lover, who was charged with the murder and freed on a technicality. He then skipped the country. Dean Olds was never indicted. Anderson filed what turned out to be a successful civil suit to prevent Olds from seizing control of the dead woman's estate.

The safest course, and often the only course, is to deliver what Anderson calls "a bland factual recitation."

Anderson also represented Illinois Governor George Ryan in his public struggle against Jim Ryan, the state attorney general, on the death-penalty clemency issue. The case would have been of great interest to TV under any circumstances, but the fact that Jim Ryan used it in his gubernatorial race guaranteed ongoing on-air coverage.

Commenting on a case to TV reporters can be a daunting and dangerous adventure. Resisting such commentary can be equally daunting, especially when you actually see your adversary spinning his or her position for the cameras. In the Olds case, "Olds himself

(Continued on page 71)

Live from Florida...

As a momentous event, not just in American political history, but in the history of the media as well, the 2000 election recount in Florida offers a myriad of lessons for crisis and media managers. Because it was a TV broadcast, the lesson on visuals was spectacularly underscored. Always communicate in visuals. Always make your visuals more powerful than the other guy's.

If Democratic voters were disenfranchised, there were no visuals to back up that contention or drive it home. By contrast, the hanging chads worked powerfully for the Republicans, adding visual absurdity as a factor influencing perceptions of the Gore complaint.

Since much of the crisis was live on TV, the Florida saga also underscored the need to pick your spokespersons well. Here again, the Republicans had a decisive upper hand.

G. Irvin Terrell, a trial counsel to President Bush and Vice President Cheney during the Florida struggle, believes an important decision was to "bifurcate" the choice of spokespersons. Former Secretary of State James Baker would speak to policy and position, reiterating essential message points about how rules cannot be changed midstream. Baker might scoff at the Democratic position, but a second spokesperson, former Montana Governor and Republican National Chairman Marc Rocicot, would be the real attack dog.

In the war of former Secretaries of State, Baker also posed a powerful contrast to Warren Christopher, a respected spokesperson for the Democrats, but not nearly as commanding or svelte as the occasion required.

Terrell, a partner at Baker Botts in Houston and a veteran of much high-profile litigation, including the Texaco/Pennzoil case of the late 1980s, believes the Democrats relied too heavily on their attorney, David Boies, whose constant media chores may have made him "less focused" on the case itself. (Uncharacteristically, Boies did not return our repeated calls for comment.)

If so, there's a lesson here for crisis planners on how trial attorneys should be deployed during litigation, especially since Boies' easy facility with the media is often held up as a paradigm for attorneys who want to maximize their client's case as well as aggressively promote themselves. If Boies was actually part of the problem, rather than the solution, for client Al Gore, the case would certainly suggest that choice of spokesperson should never be automatic.

Is there a natural flow from advocacy in the courtroom to advocacy on the courthouse steps, where reporters, not jurors, are the arbiters? If so, the trial attorney is a natural spokesperson. If not, the strategy needs to be refined.

(Continued from page 69)

was standing there everyday telling his side to the TV reporters," recalls Anderson. Part of the lawyer's job is to "deflect" media attention from the client, but in a way that keeps the reporters friendly while throwing them only the barest bones.

Toward that end, attorneys should usually explain the constraints that have been placed on them in a way that expresses professional respect for the reporters. The "my hands are tied" line is often the best you can do. For the majority of reporters, even TV reporters, that's usually enough. One reliable alternative strategy is to direct reporters to a disinterested third party for background or for commentary and attribution. By doing so, you've kept the reporter happy, while there's a good chance your surrogate will get your point of view across.

In the capital-punishment fracas, Anderson made a televised statement, with the governor's approval, accusing the attorney general of being politically motivated. The statement was aired throughout the daily news cycle.

BLACK HATS, WHITE HATS

To paraphrase Billy Crystal, "It is wonderful to be mah-velous but it is more wonderful to look mah-velous."

Remember, TV news, like TV cowboy shows or TV cop thrillers, requires good guys and bad guys. The good guys look like good guys. The bad guys look like bad guys.

Doing something about these crucial visual determinants... well, that's the tricky part. You can't change your face or your physique. In some instances, the better part of valor is to defer to another spokesperson as the TV point person. However, attorneys representing clients in high-profile cases don't usually have that option. It's part of their job to go on television.

One of the most respected criminal attorneys in the United States, Albert Krieger, offers a particularly interesting example of how to adjust a potentially damaging visual appearance and manner to the exigencies of the visual media. During the 1980s, he was a frequent presence on television as his client, one John Gotti, was tried and re-tried until finally convicted and sent to prison.

Krieger is squat-shouldered, bald, and craggy-faced. He looks like the kind of lawyer a murderer might hire. "It was something I thought about all the time," says Krieger.

Moreover, Krieger is a zealous advocate. He has strong opinions and expresses them strongly. When we joked that he was scarier on TV than his infamous client, Krieger related that in the early 1970s he had done a training video for an opening session of the National College of Criminal Defense. He was painstaking in his efforts to observe proper decorum and maintain professional gentility as he demonstrated the fine points of cross-examination.

When he saw the video for the first time, he was shocked by his own ferocity. "If this is what I am like when I'm trying to be gentle, what must I look like when I'm not! I lost a full night's sleep fretting over it."

Krieger's solution was a simple one: to use the English language well and earn the respect of reporters for the substance of his remarks. "No 'dees' and 'dems,' no street talk, just [substantive] legal sound bites," says Krieger. "There was nothing more I could do. With a careful use of language, I tried to moderate the [impression] I made."

Is that enough to impress a TV audience bound up wholly in the visuals? Probably not. But at least by impressing the reporters, Krieger avoided the trap that another one of Gotti's attorneys, Bruce Cutler, fell into when he was characterized by the media, not as a respectable criminal lawyer, but as a "legal mouthpiece."

There's no doubt the respect Krieger earned from the TV reporters carried over into their coverage and tempered the unsettling visual impact. Throughout the Gotti trials, you never heard a bad word about him.

So Don't Forget...

The rules on TV are very different, and the process considerably more dangerous. Here are three fundamental lessons for surviving broadcasts and narrowcasts:

- Refuse to comment only if you have an airtight reason to do so that actually makes you look better in the process.

- Don't elucidate substantive points for the TV cameras. No one cares. No one will get to see them anyway. Master the art of the sound bite.

- Measure the visual impact of your appearance on television. It's a visual medium. One ugly scowl can undo volumes of verbal truth.

SEVEN

Secret Weapons, Open War: Optimized Internet Strategies as a Litigation Tool

Here's an interesting experiment that C-suite executives and their legal counsel ought to conduct if only to educate themselves about the intricacies, deceptions, and pitfalls of the virtual world. Pick a high-profile corporate dispute currently in the news or about to be. Then enter the defendant's name, or the name of the company ostensibly under attack, on a popular search engine—Google, Yahoo!, or MSN will do—along with some case-related term or terms. Try a few more similar "crises" or disputes or lawsuits, and you'll note that a similar and somewhat disturbing pattern emerges.

Most of the top search results—and by "top" we mean the links that turn up highest on the search engine index—will be websites and blogs that are posted by adversarial interest groups of one sort or another. Some of these attacks are launched by Non-Government Organizations (NGOs). Some are placed by the plaintiffs' bar. Some are the product of collaboration between the two. The NGOs have ideological agendas, and are mainly interested in winning the hearts and minds of their public audiences as well as influencing journalists, regulators, and analysts. The plaintiffs' attorneys may be ideologically motivated as well, but they are keenly interested in trolling for business, setting up their next cases, testing the class action waters and soliciting class members.

The content of the websites and blogs posted by the NGOs and plaintiffs' lawyers may actually have little or nothing to do with the specific legal issue at play. Instead, they're quite likely broadside attacks aimed at the corporate bow, designed to vitiate the company's specific legal position with a more general assault on its brand. In other words, if they don't win their battles by addressing the facts of the matter—be it a crisis in consumer confidence or a major lawsuit —they do so by broadly discrediting the honesty, integrity, and corporate good citizenship of the company under attack.

Here, as elsewhere in the communications wars, plaintiffs' lawyers know what they're doing. If anything, they're getting better at it all the time. Many advocates have shrewdly learned to game the system via "Search Engine Optimization" (known as SEO), ensuring that Google, Yahoo!, and MSN find them early and often.

The adversaries have figured out what it takes to attract search engine "spiders," the mechanisms by which online postings move up on the search engine indices. They know how to identify and implant "keywords" that likewise prioritize what they post, or, at the very least, they know enough to hire someone who does.

Crusaders aren't waiting for people to find them. These activists purposefully use language and HTML code that guarantee attention from the search engines that are constantly "crawling" through the web. They understand that both content and context factor into higher search engine rankings.

Yet two can play the same proverbial game. Some site or blog has to be ranked Number One for any given high-value search phrase or keyword, so why not yours instead of theirs? Retain an experienced SEO specialist who can identify for you the words and phrases likely to be recognized as keywords by the search engines. Sprinkle the site with those keywords, but don't overdo it. It is not necessary to mangle a fluent web text simply to maximize keyword appearances, especially since there are other devices to prioritize the site for search engine users. For example, meta-tags are invisible HTML codes attached to sites. They include both the tag name itself (e.g., "Product Liability") and any brief text that may accompany it. That text can be very important, since it could be included verbatim on the search page itself. Imagine journalists searching "product liability" and finding your own language on Google, which depicts your opponent's lawsuit as "flagrantly disregarding expert studies confirming the safety" of the product.

Such potential impact on journalists—an increasingly predominant majority of whom rely on the search engines for their research, according to recent studies—suggests that SEO works best when it's part of a comprehensive and integrated Internet case strategy that includes online media relations, blog campaigns, and aggressive grassroots tactics. The point is, merely creating a website is less than half the battle, considering the seemingly infinite number of sites that are likely to elbow out anything that you may have posted even within the narrow confines of a particular industry or topic.

Getting a website *found* by search engines is the real name of the game.

A FUNDAMENTAL PROCESS

Optimized websites are crucial both before and during crises and litigation. It's smart policy under any circumstances to identify potential legal crises long before they hit. The Internet dimension of such prophylaxis is to ensure that your site is already positioned in the search engines, waiting to be found by the many thousands of open minds now seeking information.

Remember, it can take many weeks, and often months, to achieve high rank on the search engines. Waiting to the last minute to address adverse scenarios is thus a recipe for disaster. Search Engine Optimization has to be an integral part of an organization's contingency planning. Otherwise the war is over before you've even turned up on the battlefront.

At the same time, websites are an increasingly potent force once a crisis breaks in the press, or when a case does seem headed for trial or at least the courtroom steps. Aggressive websites and internet marketing strategies can help:

- Create a public mood that leads to favorable perceptions of the trial;

- influence the potential jury pool;

- dispel misinformation and disinformation; and

- persuade, not only journalists, but customers and clients, stockholders, and analysts.

The fact that lawyers and other crisis counselors can and, increasingly, must use search engine strategies to their clients' advantage was glaringly evident in a recent international patent infringement case. When the company's adversary shrewdly misinterpreted a court ruling in order to claim a specious "victory" in a complicated international litigation, the company, drawing on counsel from its lawyers and communications specialists, hit the 'net hard, working the "blogosphere" with sophisticated third-party statements reinterpreting the ruling and simultaneously optimizing the clarification.

The correct rendition, rather than their competitor's false claim, carried the day as the campaign generated 1.4 million impressions and more than 4,000 click-throughs to the decisive web page. Such numbers suggest that an overwhelming majority of the audience that had any direct interest in the case—in other words, the critical audience—did indeed read the corporate rejoinder. At the same time, similar clarifications were posted on scores of independent blogs that were already reaching readers directly interested in or affected by the dispute.

Consider another recent scenario, which we've disguised a bit to protect the innocent. One company in Asia sued another party for negligence involving a complex paper trail and the real possibility that the defendant has been malfeasant. Within two weeks of the company's site going up in optimized format, its messages were interwoven with media outreach efforts throughout the world. Before the third week was over, the breadth and depth of media penetration decisively affected discovery when the company received a call from a "deep throat" advising that certain documents establishing the malfeasance were stored in a specific location on another continent.

The Internet's global reach may be cliché, but here we see how the right website, effectively optimized, can actually incite decisive action on a multi-continent basis—even as it disseminates information across vast distances.

The benefits of optimization aren't so mysterious when one remembers that somewhere between one-half and three-quarters of all activity on the web is triggered by Google, Yahoo!, or MSN. The search engine users are earnestly looking for information. If they're often less than disinterested, they're still malleable, much like the crucial independent segment of the electorate in a political campaign. If you don't reach them, the other side will.

Finally, the benefits of websites and SEO extend beyond the duration of the case. Once your site or blog ranks high, it stays that way. It becomes an ongoing source of expert information, constantly reinforcing your message until it takes on the force of common wisdom. You can institutionalize your message with a series of "landing pages," which are short and pointed descriptions of specific issues critically important to your audiences. Each landing page is separately optimized, directing traffic to the individual page and, from there, to the rest of your site.

You have thus built a platform by which, finally, you can extend your message to other sympathetic, credible, and ostensibly disinterested sites, providing, from a communications standpoint, a permanent insulation from misinformation.

Smart organizations play both offense and defense.

So Don't Forget...

Online sources gain instantaneous credibility simply by existing. As a result, the Internet hasn't simply leveled the playing field. It has, in fact, tipped the scales in favor of the aggressor. Corporations under attack must therefore play this game as well, and the one indispensable weapon is Search Engine Optimization (SEO).

- Conduct rigorous worst-case contingency planning and prepare to play both offense and defense.

- Publish content regularly: Expert articles, newsletters, et al. Archive the content on your site and submit it to other sites, requesting a link back to your site with a proper citation for you as "author."

- Get other respected sites to link to yours, thus assuring the popular search engines that your site is credible and authoritative.

- Take extra crucial steps to ensure that your website's code and structure are search engine-friendly. While neither corporate executives nor their legal and communications advisors need to know the "how-to" details, they do need to rely on Internet experts who can guarantee that their sites meet the search engine-friendly specifications.

- Continue to maintain and optimize your site after the crisis or lawsuit is over. For example, optimized "landing pages" addressing specific issues can be added on indefinitely, further consolidating and propagating your message in the virtual universe.

EIGHT

A Whole New Ballgame: How Blogs Have Taken Crisis Communications to the Next and Unprecedented Level

"The outlook for newspapers is not great."
—Warren Buffet

"Stop the Presses." That's easy enough for us to say, but the truth is that you can never stop all the presses when everybody's got one. Today's new media pack doesn't need to buy ink by the barrel every week. They pay Internet fees instead and enlist (without qualifying degrees) in the army of opinion-shapers and world movers universally known as bloggers. An underground fourth estate now breaks stories, cremates reputations, provides authoritative data, challenges brands, defends brands, and reaches much larger audiences than most daily newspapers.

So, everything you've ever learned about crisis communications…well, thanks to blogs and the blogosphere, you can now underscore those lessons a thousand-fold. Ratchet up the sense of urgency. Exponentially increase the levels of preparedness should your company face a public challenge or be hit with a high-profile lawsuit. Be ready, as you've never been ready before, to have answers to all the tough questions that may confront you.

In case you don't know, a blog (or weblog) is a regularly updated online "journal", where people write about things they find interesting. Blogs get posted on every subject imaginable. Some bloggers are simply cranks, but that won't stop them from firing salvos at the corporate hull. Your important audiences may even use these cranks as sources of information. Meanwhile, there are "high-authority" bloggers whose opinions are sanctified by the full faith and credulity of the surfing public.

You know a high-authority blog when you see one. Is it being quoted by major industry trades? Are Harvard business professors posting there? On January 12, 2005, in *U.S. v Booker*, the Supreme Court cited the *Sentencing Law and Policy Blog*, the creation of Ohio State University Professor Douglas Berman. Now *that's* a high-authority blog!

It was an important moment, not just in American legal history, but in American history, period. The blogosphere has entered the mainstream at the highest possible level. Meanwhile, there is also a growing number of state and federal courts that reference blogs as if they were law review articles. The boundary between sanctified texts and online resources has definitely blurred.

"Our blog is read by professors from around the world, as well as antitrust enforcers and practitioners in the field," says D. Daniel Sokol, Visiting Associate Professor at the University of Missouri-Columbia School of Law and one of the authors of *Antitrust & Policy Competition*, a top-ranked blog focused on antitrust issues. "On a regular basis, reporters call about any number of antitrust-related issues. Savvy companies and their media relations professionals play a critical role in our blog by alerting us to important antitrust developments around the world."

In Chapter 11, we argue that antitrust decisions are especially subject to the influence of public opinion, since standards like "best interests of the consumer" are open to wide-ranging interpretation. Antitrust regulators, in our view, are not therefore ashamed to openly calibrate media coverage in formulating their decisions.

If your company has antitrust issues of any sort, we'd further stress how especially important it is to monitor trends and events as well as track opportunities for savvy companies to highlight any antitrust developments they want covered.

Not just issues, you must also know the high-authority bloggers relevant to your industry. You need to treat them as if they directly feed *The Wall Street Journal* because, in fact, many of them do. Industry analysts track blogs too, and it would be surprising if the regulators who oversee drugs and food and telecommunications resist the temptation. As John Mack points out, the impact of high-authority blogs like his own reaches the inner recesses of your own organization as well.

"A substantial portion—over 40%—of readers of my blog are employees of pharmaceutical companies," says Mack, Editor and Publisher of *Pharma Marketing News* and the *Pharma Marketing Blog*. "The vast majority of readers—65%—are somewhat or very supportive of the industry. Many of these people would like the industry to have a better public image and believe, as I do, that the first step in that direction is for the industry to better regulate itself.

"The opinions and revelations I make on my blog resonate with these people and suggest that the drug industry can lose support from its core—their own employees!" (See Chapter 9 for more on the challenges facing the pharmaceutical industry.)

THE DRUDGE FACTOR

Journalists are often "scooped" by bloggers and follow their lead rather than vice versa. The media has had to adapt to bloggers and, since it could not beat them, it has joined them. Blogging has provided a dynamic platform where journalists, the public, and industry people can interact and discuss issues. *The Wall Street Journal*, for example, now has fifteen blogs of its own, covering areas like health, law, the economy, and even auto shows.

(Continued on page 87)

Issues Management: The Essential Steps

You'll recall the definition of issues management that Manly Molpus provided us in Chapter 4: "Issues management is a thoughtful analysis of a potentially critical issue, with an action plan by which a point of view can be effectively advocated."

Remember, though, that the action plan must be more than a series of messages to be delivered by your industry spokespersons whenever a journalist happens to call or a blog post requires a response. Effective advocacy—the kind of effective advocacy that changes the opinions of whole populations—must be multifaceted, persistent, proactive, and aggressive. Its pieces must fit together and reinforce each other. It must be grassroots.

So, what does all that mean? While the range of tactical components is well-nigh inexhaustible, here's an introductory cookbook. You'll find some mix of these ingredients in most successful issues campaigns...

✔ Find and deploy a wide range of credible leaders—academics, experts, business leaders, community leaders, and others—who will endorse and advocate your position. Each endorsement will be a pretext for additional media coverage spread out over time.

✔ Mobilize a coalition of organizations to support your position. If there is a racial dimension, consider groups like the LULAC (League of United Latin American Citizens) or the Urban League. Perhaps AARP is an appropriate source of support in a health or benefits-related campaign. Look to such organizations that reach a broad spectrum of the public, from decision-makers to media sources to the Man and Woman in the Street.

✔ Create and attend editorial board meetings with major local and national media. If there is a legislative dimension to the campaign, a Congressman's local paper in Iowa City or Biloxi will be as influential as the major outlets. The two certainly reinforce each other. When your point of view is *simultaneously* supported by reporters in both venues, the effect on anyone who's interested in getting reelected—even as they want to seek to play a larger role on the national or international stage—is decisive.

✔ Generate a persistent, growing tide of emails, letters, and phone calls to policy-makers or other decision-makers from "ordinary citizens" in support of your goals.

✔ Look for local supporters to byline their own articles in local media. If, for example, a drug company wants to impress its point of view on a particular community, an op-ed by a respected local physician can be at least as effective as a barrage of corporate image ads. Such outreach is "grass-roots" in the truest sense. On a community by community basis, multiple articles will generate a groundswell of supportive opinion and provide fodder for use online.

✔ Launch "free media" Public Service Announcement (PSA) campaigns targeting key radio and possibly local TV outlets: News, talk, and, to be sure, programming aimed at specific groups that you need to reach. Programming aimed at minority groups, for example, are naturally prime venues in some campaigns.

✔ Publish issue ads in major media outlining the industry's position. At the same time, don't underestimate image ads not directly related to the issue at hand. During a Vioxx trial in New Orleans, for example, the judge gagged both sides. Neither could talk to the media about anything Vioxx-related. But Merck stepped up its local image ads ("meet the people of Merck") to increase public empathy for the company. The plaintiffs had no such option; there was no distinct organization for them to promote. Merck won the case.

✔ As discussed in this chapter, find and obtain endorsements from "high-authority" bloggers with influence among your target audiences. These bloggers are the ones with real credibility among the audiences you want to persuade.

✔ Conduct polls that will reinforce broad support for your position. Distribute the results to the media and further target specific audiences in the process. Such surveys can be repeated throughout the campaign. If the results of a survey do not support your position, don't disseminate the results. All you've lost is the cost of conducting the survey, while the adverse data may well be invaluable in identifying your current and persistent weaknesses.

✔ Use focus groups to increase your grasp of how the public views your issue. An abiding benefit of these groups is that they're formal enough to yield solid empirical data—but colloquial enough to allow the professionals who conduct them to identify the long-term action points and message points that either reinforce supportive opinion or influence negative opinion in your direction.

One campaign launched by a major corporation neatly underscores how issues management operates both broadly and narrowly. When Cingular Wireless sought approval from the DOJ and FCC for its acquisition of AT&T Wireless, the company aggregated support in three critical sectors: local emergency first-responders like police and fire departments; national advocacy groups for handicapped citizens; and the CEOs of wireless telecommunications firms serving rural areas.

It was thus a public interest campaign, not just a legal one. The message overwhelmed opposition from consumer advocacy organizations and unleashed a tsunami that public opinion-conscious regulators could not resist).

(Continued from page 83)

Bloggers are the on-the-ground journalists of the new media. They get press credentials to cover political conventions. They have readerships in the millions. They break news (think Mark Foley) and they keep stories alive (think Monica Lewinsky). Bloggers' and new media stories may not arrive on your doorstep like the morning paper, but technologies such as RSS (Really Simple Syndication) and bookmarks provide readers with online subscriptions that are just as reliable.

Savvy bloggers and readers won't stand for corporate rhetoric or tactical obfuscation. "Most bloggers don't respond well to marketing pitches, but we do appreciate real information," says Bruce Schneier, security technologist and author of the *Schneier on Security* blog.

Developing and implementing a substantive blogging strategy in advance of a crisis is therefore critical. A blog gives businesses a way to stay ahead of the news cycle by presenting, testing, and refining the company's message, distinguishing facts from fiction, and correcting any misinformation that may be circulating and propagating through the blogosphere.

The operative word is "substantive." As Schneier says, "the more you spin, the less we listen."

FROM RANK-AND-FILE TO THE A-LIST

Blogs first surfaced as online journals, posting random streams of consciousness that were published as online diaries. The blogosphere is still abundant with diaries, as about 37% fall into this category. But in its maturation, the online blog community is now crowded with citizen journalists, editors, and experts passionately advocating a cause, curse, or career.

Fabulous Fisherman Fred blogs side by side with CEOs from Fortune 100 companies. You'll find Fred's blogroll friends (the folks who post commentary to the blog) talking tackle and even trading bass lures. Google the Fortune 100 CEO and you'll also find the latest company successes as well as what the disgruntled IT guru is saying about the company's software migration.

The blogosphere may or may not include the voice of your legal counsel, but you can surely expect the plaintiffs' bar to troll for clients through marketing blogs. You'll find the good, the bad, and the very, very ugly. You'll often find flame sites about your company's products, exposés of "customer no-service" or allegations of dubious hiring policies, along with the latest inside information delivered in cyber-time by your competition. There are bloggers from MIT, Microsoft, and *The New York Times* among the tens of millions who generate and propagate content through the blogosphere.

But the MITs and Microsofts or mainstream media brands don't necessarily dominate the popularity-driven Blogosphere A-list. Internet storytellers rank particularly high. Most of these storytellers don't consider themselves journalists. Ask Fabulous Fisherman Fred. He might say he hates the media even if he doesn't realize that his buzz on the latest lure and its defects has trumped every other carefully placed product review. Fred can ignite media attention and shift the communications focus from product launch to the crisis scramble necessitated by product recall. *Are the lure manufacturers ready? Have they thought ahead to that eventuality?*

Bloggers like Fred and his millions of counterparts have tremendous impact by influencing the media and public opinion through what's often an anonymous no-holds-barred online debate. Blog search engine Technorati measures the global blog at about 70 million, while the number of blogs doubles every six months with 1.2 million blog posts daily. Amid such numbers, what are the odds of your company evading unwanted coverage should you face any sort of organizational crisis?

DIFFERENT GAME, DIFFERENT RULES

It is specifically because of the differences between blogs and traditional media that companies must adapt their crisis communications plan to incorporate a solid online component that takes the blogosphere as seriously as it deserves to be taken.

"The number one thing to know is not to ignore bloggers," says John Mack. "A story may live for a short time in the media, but never dies within the interconnected blogosphere. If PR people do not engage bloggers, their voices are not heard in this sphere, which is having greater and greater impact on the public."

As Mack says, unlike traditional editorial content, blogs have a shelf life that far surpasses media coverage, not to mention the messages originating from your own official company web site. In fact, information on blogs lives indefinitely, giving last year's blog attack a weight equal to today's positive media spin and the recent press release added to your online newsroom. You simply have to scroll down to find it. By contrast, yesterday's newspaper is now wrapped around the remains of last night's dinner. Traditional editorial content lasts only as long as the newspaper sits on the table or the six o'clock news program is on the air.

Meanwhile, blog archival content arises in search results over and over again via "permalink" technology and can be reposted and redistributed again and again. Blog content remains relevant long after information has moved from the home page of the blog, and long after yesterday's headlines are replaced with today's online news.

"The Internet speeds up the dissemination of not only information but also misinformation," says Jeff Jarvis, who heads the interactive journalism program at the CUNY Graduate School of Journalism and blogs on journalism and media at *Buzzmachine.com*. "So what are we to do about this? Regulate? Legislate? Complain? Ignore? Respond?

"We need to recognize that the Internet alters how media operate," adds Jarvis. "Blogs—whether written by professionals or amateurs—tend to publish first and edit later, which can work because the audience will edit you. In this medium, stories are never done; rather than turning into fish-wrap, they can grow and become more factual and gather new perspectives, thanks to the power of the link and, yes, the correction."

Blogs have other legs-up as well. Affiliation is easy to mask and bloggers can be completely anonymous. Unlike editorial content in the mainstream media, the citizen journalist may be unknown. There's a good chance that, if a blogging activist is badmouthing your company, you may never know that person's true identity.

In addition, while mainstream journalists meet midnight deadlines and move on, bloggers remain vigilant in the background and delve beyond the surface scoop. They're not limited by the competitive platform of media as a business or the 24-hour news cycle. Bloggers talk. They're connected. They match wits, offer references, trade information, and share sources and resources.

They pursue doggedly and they pursue endlessly. Their identity (or lack thereof) is not in their names, but resides in, and is validated by, the hyperlinks that justify their analysis and opinion. Who they are pales in comparison to the credibility of the information they unearth and deliver, which often becomes a bona fide transparent media source.

Many bloggers police their counterparts and other media; they're adept in surfacing and connecting information that the press corps has missed. Despite amateur status or anonymity, these investigators and their networks can quickly shift yesterday's ground-zero headlines into a frenzied media groundswell.

A NIMBLE ADVERSARY

There are few barriers to entry when it comes to blogging. Low-cost or no-cost blogging software is widely available, making it extremely easy for people to publish, regardless of technological skill. Bloggers make the most of this "think it, write it, publish it" technology, reacting to breaking news and current events with judgment calls, personal opinions, and links to additional sources offered in real time. After all, bloggers have no legal department, corporate communications bureaucracy, copy desk, or executive chain of command. There's nothing to slow them down; the "approval process" starts with the blog post—be it rant, rave, ramble, or vent—and the real-time buzz is measured by audience response, reaction, and viral circulation.

Blogs may not seem as official as the 30-second sound bite or as memorializing as the primetime news spot that encapsulated your take on Katrina or food contamination, a fatal train derailment or the potential consequences of a hazardous waste spill. Perhaps you had the last word or potentially will. And, you might think, blog buzz could never come close to the dividends your company expects from the upcoming *BusinessWeek* interview. Well, consider what *BusinessWeek* itself had to say (May 2, 2005):

> "Go ahead and bellyache about blogs. But you cannot afford to close your eyes to them, because they're simply the most explosive outbreak in the information world since the Internet itself. And they're going to shake up just about every business—including yours. It doesn't matter whether you're shipping paper clips, pork bellies, or videos of Britney in a bikini, blogs are a phenomenon that you cannot ignore, postpone, or delegate. Given the changes barreling down upon us, blogs are not a business elective. They're a prerequisite. (And yes, that goes for us, too.)"

If media relations are a two-way street, then blogs suggest four-way intersections. While editorial and traditional media present information, blogs toss it in the sandbox as fact or fiction and invite everyone to play. The information will live or die in these lively interactive forums of discussion and idea exchange. Traditional media, along with traditional concepts of damage control, do not compass these whirligigs of content and perception-sharing. Barriers and boundaries between what's public and what's private have dissolved in a ubiquitous medium that challenges the traditional information gatekeepers and those formerly quoted as industry experts.

HOW TRADITIONAL MEDIA USE BLOGS

It's no wonder that mainstream media have joined the blogosphere. After ignoring its power of persuasion, the media itself now blogs because of revenue, influence, and because mainstream and emerging audiences go online for news and almost everything else. Perhaps the growing number of media blogs is evidence of the media's desire to be part of this larger conversation.

This morning's blog post may be the catalyst for tomorrow's front-page headline. As information, news, opinions, speculation, misinformation, and propaganda move through the blogosphere at the speed of light, reporters are looking to blogs for alternative angles and tracking their hyperlinked research into news-making stories. Consider:

- ✔ Blogs played a catalytic role in the 2006 Mark Foley sex scandal, revealing the first IM messages.

- ✔ Blogs were credited with helping interest mainstream news in the racially insensitive remarks by Senator Trent Lott that led to his resignation as Senate Majority Leader.

- ✔ Bloggers first sent up the alarm about the forged Bush/National Guard memos reported as authentic by Dan Rather, a debacle for CBS and *60 Minutes*.

- ✔ During the Virginia Tech tragedy, blogs and social media offered real-time interviews and images that were integrated as part of CNN reports. While *Roanoke Times* journalists used online blog formats for their coverage, other mainstream media scoured blogs and forums for eyewitness sources.

- ✔ The real truth behind Starbucks' earnings shortfall was a few forecasts short, revealed popular *StarbucksGossip.com*. The company told Wall Street the story, but the blog told it the rest of the story. It linked the news to predictions from the blogger's own Main Street audience of store managers.

Those store managers said they had forecast losses and shared their concerns with company chiefs eight months earlier.

But, not all media rank-and-file are believers. Joseph Rago, an Assistant Editorial Features Editor at *The Wall Street Journal*, wrote an editorial (December 20, 2006) in which he opined that blogs are "written by fools to be read by imbeciles." Bloggers had a field day. One response was offered the very next day by a blogger who calls his blog *Texas Hold 'Em:*

Be Blog-less at Your Peril

Over a 10-day period, Kryptonite Locks, the world's leading bike lock manufacturer, found out the hard way what happens when bloggers are ignored. After bloggers identified a problem with the security of a particular Kryptonite lock, they posted a video of how to easily open one with a common ballpoint pen. The story traveled through the blogosphere as Kryptonite spent ten days struggling to get its messaging and online strategy together—a veritable lifetime or two on the Internet. In the meantime, *The New York Times* picked up the story.

Kryptonite staffers were aware of the blogosphere activity. They knew that the lock in question was indeed vulnerable and they were working out a plan to correct the defect. But they never effectively used online media to disseminate their side of the story. Seven days after the story broke, they hadn't even updated their own web site with information about the situation. Ten days after the first forum post, the company announced that lock owners could exchange defective locks for free.

The cost to Kryptonite? A bruised reputation and about $10 million. Yet as of September 1, 2007, Kryptonite Locks still has no blog.

"…Rago's words bring to mind the old saw about media elitism: 'Here's the news and here's what to think about it…' This condescending attitude is precisely what led to the rise of alternative media, such as cable news, talk radio, the Internet and blogs… Blogs here in Wisconsin and across the nation have influenced local, state and even national stories. Quick: how was the chairman of the Racine County Democratic Party forced to resign in light of sexual harassment? A blog—*RealDebate Wisconsin.* The traditional media—*Racine Journal Times* and *Milwaukee Journal*—arrived at the party late…How did Senior McGee eventually have to face disciplinary action for telling racist jokes on the airwaves? How did news of Junior McGee saying Leon Todd should be [hanged] break? It wasn't the *Milwaukee Journal* but rather *Badger Blogger* in both cases…"

This rejoinder certainly supports the more scientific finding of a Columbia University study that shows 51% of journalists use blogs regularly. The number is rapidly growing, in large part because, for all the abuses and misinformation, they provide real value. "In many ways, blogs keep the media honest," says Bruce Schneier. "Far too often, the established media presents stories in easy-to-digest hard-to-offend nuggets. Bloggers look beyond those nuggets to the real story.

"Yes, there's an echo chamber where certain views get magnified and others get ignored," adds Schneier. "But the established media does that too, to an even more extreme degree. Think of blogs as the final democratization step of the media revolution begun with the invention of the printing press. Embrace the fact that you can't control the story, and let the facts speak for themselves.

"Sure, it's not what you want but it's way better than you'll get otherwise," says Schneier.

A CORPORATE RESOURCE

During a recent PR Newswire forum on blogs, David Whelan, a staff writer at *Forbes* and a blog fan, commented that blogs "give you an idea of what opinions are out there before you pick up the phone." He noted that companies that have blogs are going to be noticed more because lots of story ideas "bubble up" from blogs to the mainstream media.

The ideal proactive campaign begins with a blog that is already in place. It is a transparent extension of your company's brand and communications, a way to develop and grow customer and audience relationships. It is clear, real, and authentic because it really is a conversation, and a transparent one at that. The blog voices talk in plain language, dispensing with the stiff formality often found in press releases (which are intended for the media but often stumbled on by customers searching online).

Blogs give companies a place to talk and listen as well as a lively, alternative platform to post insights, articles, news, and comments on industry happenings. The blog can easily cement your position as an industry thought leader. You'll know because your insights will circulate rampantly as permalinks in the blogging global arena. At the same time, the ideal blog is more than an alternative forum to roll out the latest news brief, extol the internal mechanisms of your company, or tout support for its business objectives. It is also about its people—their concerns and connections to the world inside and outside the company.

Because the blog already exists, it will presumably have a ready audience that will turn to it if the company becomes a topic of public conversation, especially negative conversation. They will naturally want to know what you have to say in response to whatever it is that Badget Blogger said about you. And, it should be optimized—see Chapter 7 for more on this crucial procedure—to attract the greatest number of additional web users.

Used proactively, blogs give companies a way to test, manage, and actually "experience" the messages in front of their audiences—and with their audiences—and this experience includes both the messages the company intends and those "outside" messages the audience will certainly hear. In that sense, a blog can be a tool for a company to go on the offensive: To disseminate its messages before those messages are needed in response to an allegation or criticism. It is a way for the company to define the debate in the blogosphere before it even begins.

Beyond that, you will need to be constantly monitoring the blogosphere to assess how your proactive measures are being received and, certainly, to identify areas where you are being attacked and don't yet know it.

Which takes us to the crucial nuts and bolts of what corporations really must deliver in this brave and frequently capricious new world.

THE BRASS TACKS

It's often observed that a person who has a good experience tells one other person; a person who has a bad experience tells five. The blogosphere underscores this truism, whether the telling originates as a competitor's flame attack, as comment from a dissatisfied customer, or as the personal blog opinion of an unhappy employee blasting a management initiative. You'll be hard-pressed to prevent the spread of misinformation. From a practical standpoint, much of it won't justify a response. Nevertheless, your blog is a way to tap the pulse of the blogosphere and, when warranted, respond appropriately to inaccuracies or damaging messages before they land on a high-authority blog and then proliferate uncontrollably.

If you've got a computer or gaming system in your house, you probably have at least one or two Electronic Arts (EA) video games. But as savvy as the company is in game design, they didn't quite realize the technological power of the blogosphere. They learned the hard lessons of online buzz when a blogger called EA Spouse posted about the working conditions at EA. She wasn't complimentary.

What started out as a single post on a relatively insignificant blog rapidly gained momentum and, in short order, media attention. When mainstream media asked EA for comment on the online allegations, EA's response was the one we've all been trained to give: "We can't discuss employee issues." Alas, the *EA Spouse* blog is, to this day, highly ranked in Google, while EA recently settled a $15 million overtime suit brought against it by employees.

The good news is that a blog threat isn't necessarily just one or two opinions posted online. Instead, these opinions, however nasty, are actually corporate assets, the early alerts needed to address (as was true in EA's case) crucial internal issues *before* external issues arise that pose more significant threats. Choose your buzz: A company blog? Or the buzz of media and public opinion that follow an employee uprising and crisis headlines?

The first step must therefore be a dedicated daily monitoring program—in fact, twice a day. From there a strategy evolves. Among the key elements of that strategy…

✔ Know what people are saying about your company. Perhaps they're commenting on a new initiative or reacting to a recent advertising campaign. Maybe they think your recent YouTube video is absolute genius. Or maybe Sue crowed about her raise in her online diary and Bill down the hall is furious. He's uploaded a litigious memo to his blog….

✔ Connect the dots. Gather information and links from a variety of company sources. Keep the information current and spread "information packages" with blog excerpts and supportive hyperlinks. The goal is that, when other bloggers descend on your blog, you want them to discover at least one part of a story that satisfies their quest to create a broader whole. The more parts you provide, the better.

✔ Use your blog to influence other blogs. With your own blog firmly in place, you'll have more credibility in the blogosphere. Your value is more than being one among many; it's in being a dynamic member of a proud community. That value and credibility extend to your links. Bloggers link—it's what they do. So give them plenty to link to.

✔ Reach out to bloggers and develop an authentic, transparent relationship with them in much the same way your corporate communications team cultivates and interacts with any influential reporter who covers your industry. Promote your relationships and connections with a "blogroll," the community of online friends and supporters.

✔ If and when a genuine crisis develops, you respond quickly through your blog, offering conversational information that's also embodied in the company's talking points, position statement, and official press release. If you're credible, embedded context links and your own blog post permalink will carry more weight and propagate more quickly than all other methods combined. Your blog news will also hang around far longer, especially if your crisis strategy deploys a commentary or link campaign.

✔ Keep your friends close and your enemies closer, as Sun-tzu, the Chinese philosopher and military strategist, advised. A blog monitor will help your business identify blogging adversaries and allies before a crisis calls you to the war room, so that you can respond accordingly and, if needed, proactively. Being aware of adversity is important. Equally crucial is early knowledge of loyalty and support. You may need to mobilize allied forces to broadcast your message. Messages have greater weight when third parties deliver them.

✔ You'll also want to identify bloggers who are likely to start or circulate rumors or jump on a cause about your overall industry as well as those bloggers who are neutral or objective.

A monitor that analyzes allies and enemies, and the early-warning systems and neutral camps on the periphery, can rapidly scale to an incredibly persuasive blog campaign when a crisis demands high-speed and high-stakes deployment.

A CRISIS COMMUNICATIONS TOOL

As noted, a blog that is already in place provides an immediate source for people to see how your company is reacting to rumor or news. It's faster than a press release, more conspicuous than a website update, much quicker than getting an op-ed piece in *The New York Times*, and more credible than a full-page ad in *The Washington Post*.

Silence is Leaden

Often in this book we remind our readers that "no comment" will, at best, cede the playing field to your adversaries and, at worst, constitute an admission of guilt. In the blogosphere, no-comments can be even more detrimental, especially since, in this medium, everything is archived in perpetuity, easily accessible and frequently re-circulated.

Don't listen to us. Listen to the blogosphere's guru of gurus.

"Never expect bloggers to do fact-checking or original reporting. Not even me," says Robert Scoble, the Microsoft blogging pioneer who with Shel Israel wrote the acclaimed business blogging book *Naked Conversations* (John Wiley & Sons, 2006). "But if a blog survives 24 hours without anyone refuting the facts? That's when rumors turn to belief."

"Lately I've been telling people that I start out very skeptical about what I read in blogs and my skepticism goes down after 24 hours," says Scoble. "I find that, if something untrue is reported on blogs, the company usually lets the blogosphere know (and they should). But, if something is true? They stay quiet."

Online crisis communications draws on the best practices of both proactive and reactive strategies. For example:

✔ **Say something.** Even a minimized response of "we're looking into it" can be a reassuring message of acknowledgement without any confession of liability. Meanwhile, you've bought time to assess online impact, rally legal counsel, explore blog strategy, and strategize with the entire crisis communications team.

✔ **Pre-plan.** Since at least 51% of media use blogs, contribute to theirs and invite them to use yours *before* a crisis occurs. Include real-time media updates via blog RSS feeds and encapsulated friendly versions of the company press room. When time is of the essence, key media are already trained to check your blog and rely on it as a source for official information. They also have an existing relationship with you. As in all crisis management, relationships are crucial.

✔ **Preempt.** The goal is to get a smear campaign that starts in the blogosphere to end in the blogosphere. Your clarification, and the conversations surrounding it, may be all journalists need to fact-check for the more accurate story or disregard it altogether (as a veiled flame attack from a disgruntled competitor, for example). The journalist may move on to the next rumor or discover a bigger and better story. Reporters do research rumors, but they're also looking to blogs for new angles and nuggets that can make positive company headlines too.

✔ **Humanize.** Blogs help put a human face on the organization. Personable voices enrich the corporate profile. Solid customer connections go a long way toward building loyalty when headlines are good, and empathy when the news play is crisis.

UNCOMMON COMMON SENSE

A great deal of blogosphere management requires what seems to be common sense. But, as with crisis and media management in general, such common sense is rooted in instincts. The reputation disasters that have befallen corporate America in recent years prove that those instincts are by no means universal or easily acquired.

For example, some corporations find it very difficult to sound credible when they're trying to sound human. They should study the example of Bryan Zmijewski, founder and main blogger at microstock photo site *LuckyOliver.com*, who says he's used his company's blog to share good news as well as apologize for technical snafus.

"We've heard from our customers that one of the things they really love about our business is that they can tell from our blog and our website that we're real human beings and that we care and feel real passion for what we're doing," says Zmijewski. "It's gotten to the point that, if someone is questioning our company or putting LuckyOliver in a less than positive light on another blog or in a forum, our customers actually speak out on our behalf without any prompting by us. Our blogging has played a huge role in how they feel about us."

A blog cannot sound as if it is written by a robot, a computer, or a corporation's legal department (even if it has to go through legal before it is posted). Blogs need to have the tone and personality of the people who are writing them. Think about a presentation one might give at an industry conference. It's like a formal paper, but the conversation that takes place in the hallways between sessions is like a blog post. A blog post should have a conversational tone and—this cannot be emphasized too strongly—corporations need to give their blog writers a certain leeway that they would not usually give in other corporate formats. If your bloggers want to use the word "damn," let them.

Honesty is another form of uncommon common sense that the blogosphere demands. So be transparent. If your PR firm is writing the blog on your behalf, say so. If you are posting a complimentary piece on a company that just happens to be a partner or affiliate, disclose the relationship. Scheme to be anything but completely upfront, and it's only a matter of time before the bloggers will delight in "outing" you.

Maybe that's the best news coming out of the blogosphere. As bizarre as this environment may be, your success in it depends on your humanity, your honesty, and your willingness to communicate. Those are prime qualities to feature under any circumstances.

So Don't Forget...

The blogosphere is a shoot-from-the-hip medium into which corporations are often thrust by crisis. Under daunting circumstances, it's naturally harder to identify and implement the tactical best practices. Here are a few basic ones...

- Monitor all mentions of your company in the blogosphere. Even if you don't respond, the repository of public and even internal opinion is invaluable. Information is power.

- Update the blog at least weekly and more often if possible. The denizens of the blogosphere expect you to take their medium as seriously as they do.

- Diversify your communicators. CEO blogs are great but, for journalists, valuable communications also come from the rank-and-file and lower-level managers.

- Set boundaries. Predetermine what's acceptable, especially where there's legal exposure. Talk to your lawyer but make sure your blog doesn't read like you just talked to your lawyer.

- Allow comments. One-way blogs are decisively less credible. You can restrict comments until you've reviewed them but think about publishing negative ones as well. It will show that your blog is a true public resource. It will also allow you to publicly respond to negative opinions that are probably circulating anyway.

NINE

Food, Drugs, and Money: Communications in an Age of Heightened Regulatory Activity

In today's world, every industry is a "heavily regulated industry."

Pre-Enron, the activities of federal and local regulators naturally affected all sorts of businesses and, of course, public companies and companies intending to go public. The government has long imposed rules governing Wall Street, beginning one day eight decades ago when President Roosevelt decided that Joseph Kennedy would be a shrewd, if counter-intuitive, choice to oversee the fledgling Securities and Exchange Commission.

Yet, the regulatory glare historically shone brightest on those industries dealing in products and services that have the greatest direct impact on public safety and the nation's infrastructure: Airlines, food, drugs, and telecommunications, among others. Then the spotlight changed with the corporate scandals. The SEC intensified multi-level oversight in response to new legislation driven by the very real possibility that our financial system itself was at risk.

It was a palpable mood change that carried over to other agencies as well. The ostensible failures of the private sector to adequately police itself have green-lighted regulators and prosecutors at every level of government. Never mind how pro-business some elected officials may appear. There is also a permanent government now engaged in an ongoing tug of war with corporations, while a global economy ensures that multinational companies home-officed on every continent are likewise affected.

In this environment, there's every possibility that you may have to answer to federal or local law enforcement agencies, as well as become a target of the myriad of regulatory entities that watch over the U.S. business community. The additional burden is that these government activities are often of significant public interest. As a result, reputations get damaged irrespective of how the investigations eventually resolve.

Consider the law firm that provided a disinterested opinion to Enron. Their work was limited and the opinion they provided was legally sound. None of the lawyers ever met Lay or Skilling or Fastow, yet the firm spent the next two years justifying itself to the government while trying to explain away media coverage that lumped it together with Enron's primary legal advisors.

Consider the company that unleashed a series of press releases accusing the FTC of violating its First Amendment rights. The attendant publicity was beneficial in the short run. The company got a lot of attention and increased sales. But public interest in the story eventually died. The FTC's interest did not. Now the legal entanglements continue on with no foreseeable benefit to anyone but the regulators.

In some cases, the regulators, eager to demonstrate their commitment to the public interest, will take steps to maximize media attention and shareholder awareness beyond their obligatory press releases. Their media initiatives may range from deep-throat sourcing for reporters to TV news appearances by the regulators themselves.

In a few instances, the regulatory strategies directly feed plaintiffs' lawyers filing suits as well as the ideological attacks by NGOs, even where there may be no direct communications link between them. As such, every regulatory event is a potential media event. The story may die on the vine, but that's not an assumption you can afford to safely make.

This chapter provides guidance on handling the stories that do not die on the vine. We'll discuss the planning and implementation of communications strategies during high-impact regulatory investigations—and then focus in on the challenges facing two particularly exposed industries. For the food and pharmaceutical industries, just about every regulatory crisis is a public crisis, and vice versa.

MOMENT OF TRUTH

Crisis management often hinges on a single strategic decision—do we or do we not fight back and, if so, how aggressively? It's a decision that's particularly germane when companies are grappling with the public dimension of regulatory entanglements. On the one hand, the company must protect its reputation. On the other hand, every press release, every media interview, every blog posted in the company's self-defense can alienate regulators at a point in time when it might still be possible to minimize the fallout from their investigations.

An offense communicates strength and confidence in your position. It may even convince the regulators that their own political and personal goals—more on those later—will be disserved by pursuing an inquiry that the public perceives to be unfair, bureaucratic, and arbitrary. That public influences the legislators who, in turn, oversee and fund the regulators. But the risks of going on the offense are considerable. Not only might you infuriate the regulators and intensify their zeal, an offense can generate unwanted public attention that would not otherwise have been aroused.

A defense buys time, allowing you to cooperate with the regulators and perhaps earn their trust. The risk is that you cede control of the "story" to your potential adversary. You may by your docility encourage the public's assumption that you are indeed at fault to one degree or another. That said, the abiding benefit of a defensive strategy is that it need not be permanent. If the situation deteriorates to a point where the regulators seem uncompromisingly hostile, you can launch an offense at that point. By contrast, the decision to go on the offense is usually irreversible. It's awfully hard to mend fences once you question the agency's decisions in public.

How then do you make such a decision? What factors should drive it?

First, there is nowhere such obvious need for the full and equitable collaboration of lawyers and communications professionals on the crisis team. The media strategy must be fully coordinated with the legal strategy. The company cannot be saying one thing to the regulators *in camera* and something different to *The Wall Street Journal* in public.

It's the job of the team to do risk/benefit analyses at every juncture, all the more so because the decision to stay on defense or go on offense determines every subsequent tactical action. Should you talk to the newswires? You will reach the broadest possible audience, but you won't be able to control what they write. Should you limit the offense to your own blog and thereby maintain control? You will stay in control, but you will be perceived as proportionately less credible for doing so.

Second, it's not just a question of the fact patterns underlying your particular situation. To make the decision for defense or for offense, you also need to understand who the regulators are and what they really want to accomplish. Understand that the professionals who staff these agencies are as talented as anyone in the private sector. As lawyers, they're probably equal to your own legal counselors. The regulators also believe in what they're doing. They believe they are helping the public, which can make them all the more resolute.

To that end, regulators often choose targets that allow them to send a deterring message—but they can only do that if the message is publicized. As such, media savvy is part of the regulator's job description. Whether you opt for the defense or the offense, you will need to counter their media skills with savvy of your own.

Before You Do Anything...

Once you've determined that your company is the target of a regulatory inquiry and you've gathered the basic facts, it is then critical to advise all important shareholders, investors, and key business partners.

Tell them the investigation is happening, that you will provide updates as you learn more, that you will resolve the problem as expeditiously as possible, and that the chief executive of the company is available to answer their questions.

The rule is: No surprises! Whatever your vital shareholders hear, they should hear it from you first.

DEFENSE, DEFENSE

If you are in a defensive posture, the goal is to be as cooperative as possible. It may be in the regulators' own interest to resolve the investigation expeditiously, in which case the two sides can act in full synch on the communications front as well as the legal front.

It's a fortunate position that companies should naturally want to maximize. To that end:

✔ Simply asking the agency to pre-approve company communications will show an elevated level of cooperativeness on your end.

✔ It's in your interest to defend yourself and simultaneously make the government *look good too*. Perhaps the regulator can be quoted in company press releases or online in a way that highlights his or her vigilance.

✔ Joint communiqués or press releases are possible if the company is not a direct target of the investigation or inquiry. Such communiqués remind the public that the company is, in fact, a participant and not a target.

✔ Third-party supporters may be available, including individuals whose opinions are respected by the regulators. The potential impact is obvious, especially if your allies have influence in Congress, which, as we've noted, is a high-impact audience for all regulatory agencies.

✔ Maintain a consistently positive tone and content. Any resentment or outrage will undermine the rapprochement and could even be interpreted by the government as a sign of guilt. You're on a first date, so don't be rude.

How Not To Deal With Regulators...

When Freddie Mac was investigated for accounting irregularities, Franklin Raines, then chairman and CEO of Fannie Mae, saw it as a wonderful excuse for a press conference. As reporters scribbled and cameras flashed, Mr. Raines proclaimed that such problems could never happen at his organization. Over at the Office of Federal Housing and Enterprise Oversight, a bunch of regulators pricked up their ears.

As of this writing, Mr. Raines and his colleagues are being sued for more than $200 million over alleged irregularities that were never supposed to have happened at their organization.

Such strategies are based on the assumption that a satisfactory agreement with the regulators is in the offing. When in doubt, the safer bet is to stay on the defensive and let the regulators play out whatever public scenario satisfies their short-term goals, even if there's some short-term loss for you in the Court of Public Opinion.

Again, the ongoing risk/benefit analyses worked out with your legal and communications advisors should underscore the significant risk of launching a counter-offensive prematurely. The other side can afford to fight a war of attrition that can be revivified at any time in the future, long after the matter at hand has ended and an altogether new inquiry begun.

The problem, of course, is in knowing at what point the situation is irretrievable. Some bluster on the part of the government may just be posturing, and not actually be a declaration of war. In that case, the best bet is to still play it safe. Perhaps the problem that has attracted the regulators can be isolated to one or two errant or incompetent executives. In such cases, your lawyers will advise if simply firing those executives will suffice to distance the company as a whole from an evolving investigation or, as is more likely, what level of cooperation and participation in their investigation will serve to make you the regulators' partner instead of their target.

The same strategy, of *making the requisite sacrifice*, can likewise appease multiple jurors in the Court of Public Opinion. For the media, for shareholders and analysts, for internal audiences, the message is that the problem has been solved and that the company helped the regulators solve it. You can move on now!

GO FIGHT CITY HALL

Under the worst circumstances, however, the regulators are simply out for blood. They've got you set up for a perp walk and, whatever the risks of an aggressive counter-attack, inaction is worse—the equivalent of *nolo contendere*. In such situations, flattery will get you nowhere. The regulators certainly won't listen to your joint communications proposals. And third-party supporters won't impress them unless it's a politician who happens to have assigned power over the agency.

If the government's game is to use you as a symbol for larger iniquitous trends, the best response is to beat the government at its own game by pointing to the even larger, even more iniquitous trends inherent in its actions. Those trends, which comprise the key messages of the counter-offensive, have the added advantage of speaking to issues that go far beyond the specific problems that incited the interest of the regulators in the first place. They also inspire third-party support from every imaginable quarter: politicians, other businesses, academics, and even NGOs. (For more on offense as an overall communications strategy, see Chapter 14.)

The counter-offensive thus diverts attention from the alleged corporate misdeeds by focusing on something far more important. Message points include:

✔ The government's overreaching is one more example of the ill effects of Enron and the other corporate scandals. The worst legacy of those scandals is that they have now green-lighted the government to do nearly anything it wants to do.

✔ A government out of control is far more dangerous than any of the private sector problems that it is investigating. It's called the Law of Unintended Consequences.

✔ Have the regulators reneged on any agreements? If so, they have stomped on a fundamental American value—namely, keeping one's word.

✔ From a practical standpoint, the government's ill-advised zeal muddies its relationships with other businesses with which they are negotiating, or from which they are seeking help. In so doing, they are making themselves less effective as regulators.

✔ Foreign companies are watching. If the regulators are not just aggressive but unreasonable, they are sending a negative message to global investors and thereby jeopardizing American jobs.

✔ Foreign companies are watching. For foreign businesses that are themselves facing the brunt of overzealous U.S. regulators, the sword cuts two ways. If American officials can treat a foreign company unreasonably, why can't foreign officials do the same to an American corporation?

Such a counter-offensive draws on both moral/political principles and economic self-interest, thus appealing to the most diverse possible audiences. Importantly, it is a true *offense* in the sense that it's the company and not its adversary that is setting the agenda and defining the content of the debate.

That's what an offense is supposed to do.

FOOD CRISES: AN ACUTE CHALLENGE

Nowhere is closure a more desired objective among both companies and their consumers than with food crises. In the summer of 2006, an outbreak of E.coli tainted the spinach crop, killing at least three people and sickening hundreds. On March 20, 2007, the press was still reporting an absence of resolution. These samples from coverage in the *Kansas City Star*—a heartland American newspaper—are, with our emphases added, illustrative of how a crisis can drag on with no closure in sight for a worried industry and its public.

"Despite an **unprecedented** investigation over the last six months, federal and state health officials said Tuesday that it is unlikely they will ever pinpoint the exact cause...

"The disclosure...came at a hearing where **representatives from consumer groups and a national trade association for the produce industry called on the U.S. Food and Drug Administration** to set mandatory rules to assure that fruit and vegetables are safe to eat...

"Growing and packing practices need to improve, said Dr. David Acheson, the chief medical officer for the FDA's food safety office. But he also warned that **another outbreak of food-borne illness will likely occur...**

"...farmers would like to know how the contamination occurred so they can reduce the chance of it happening again.

"...This was the **first time** investigators have been able to trace an outbreak of foodborne illness to a single field, but **they couldn't determine exactly how the bacteria came into contact with the spinach.**

"A spokesman for a major trade association also called on the FDA to impose mandatory rules for growers and packagers nationwide. James Gorny, a vice president for the United Fresh Produce Association, which represents large produce firms, **praised the efforts undertaken so far by government and industry.** But he said his group believes the only way to restore consumer confidence is for the federal government to set consistent standards and enforce them."

Such coverage is particularly interesting to a neutral observer because, while it may suggest a few failures on the part of the government and the industry to get out their message, the article is also instructive for a number of salutary crisis management steps that have apparently been taken. It's important to realize that a serious food issue like this one cannot be glibly wrapped up and buried away with yesterday's tabloids. Nor can crisis management create solutions that don't in fact exist, or provide information that is simply not available.

The fact that the investigation is depicted as "unprecedented" is a double-edged sword. It speaks well of the government and the industry that they would respond so aggressively. But it also underscores the ominous factors at work here. For all their best efforts, they still don't know, they still can't reassure. The expert source confirms the fears, generalized beyond spinach. It's good news that the illness was traced to the source, but bad news that no one knows how the infestation could have occurred.

Interestingly, the story shows a fundamental twist on the industry/regulatory interactions discussed earlier in this chapter. The industry is calling on the FDA to do more. It is not the target of a government probe and the relationship is almost collaborative. We say "almost" because one surmises a complex dance going on between the two sides, mutually supportive but with a subtle effort by the industry to maintain a separate positioning for itself.

Assuming that the story won't go away, and can't be made to go away in the near future, the mixed messages in the above coverage—in a heartland newspaper reaching a heartland audience—suggests a few strategic directions for the future:

✔ Any information that is forthcoming at any time should be immediately provided to the public as a sign of progress. If closure is not in the offing, the communications strategy needs to pursue another goal, which is to remind the public that every day brings us closer to a solution, and that that solution will indeed be found.

✔ To underscore progress, state the problem and then reassure with good news. For the published story above, the ideal message would have been (1) how the bacteria came into contact is unknown BUT (2) it is the first time that investigators succeeded in tracing the outbreak to a single field. Unfortunately, the article conveys the messages in the opposite order. When framing crisis messages, the difference is subtle and powerful. You want to get out the bad news fast and then hammer home the good news—not vitiate your good news in the very next sentence.

✔ The industry, simply by calling on the FDA to do more, is taking a leadership role and becoming a part of the solution. The earlier that role is assumed, the better, if consumer confidence is to be fully regained.

✔ The industry is taking great care to praise the government as it calls on the FDA to take further steps. No doubt such delicacy is an important part of that industry/regulatory "dance" that we have surmised.

AUSPICIOUS START

Because the E.coli crisis was not the first such event, and nor will it be the last, the industry was facing adversaries even before the revelations of contamination were made. Special interest groups and self-appointed watchdogs were lying in wait. Their lair is the blogosphere.

(Continued on page 115)

Food Crises: Names Reassure— and So Does Action

Crises such as the 2007 spinach E.coli and pet food disturbances are exceptional. Indeed, the food industry has every reason to be upbeat in its communications with the American public.

The problem is expectations. Americans want absolute safety, which wasn't possible even before the current flood of Chinese products into the U.S. market. That flood will not abate. For example, 80% of Vitamin C nutriments sold in this country now derives from China. The global dimension certainly exacerbates the communications challenge, as was evident during the pet food crisis when the fatal addition of melamine to the product was traced to China.

From a communications standpoint, it's a daunting combination. On the one hand, the public demands absolute safety and can't get it. On the other hand, the vagaries of global trade discomfort the public in general and especially with respect to China.

Even as they publicly reassert the essential integrity of the food supply, the food industry and the FDA can no longer avoid some sort of acknowledgement that "there are no absolute guarantees," says industry consultant Peter Kovacs, principal of The Kovacs Advisory Group and, from 1994 to1997, the President of NutraSweet Kelco Co.

Kovacs is fairly critical of the food industry's failure to communicate on a number of fronts. There is, for instance, a failure to use specific, credible, and reassuring language that underscores current safeguards. The industry self-enforces a regimen called "Good Manufacturing Practices" (GMP), which should be as familiar a phrase as "USDA Inspected." When GMP standards are violated, Kovacs urges use of the term "rogue event" to reaffirm the difference between business as usual and the occasional, if inevitable, problem.

Language like "rogue event" has the additional benefit of casting a villain in the crisis, which, as we saw in the classic Johnson & Johnson Tylenol scare, is mightily advantageous when companies need public support. During the pet food crisis, FDA spokesperson Stephen Sundlof announced that "somebody may have added melamine to the wheat gluten in order to increase what appears to be the protein level. Wheat gluten is a high-protein substance and by trying to artificially inflate the protein level, it could command a higher price."

According to Kovacs, Sundlof's careful but clear statement "immediately defined the problem." It was helpful on two scores. First, it established a "rogue event." Second, it limited the bad actor to "somebody" in a way that does not encourage panic over the fact that Chinese imports are now a way of life.

Less useful was the attention paid to the visit to China by U.S. inspectors. "It took six weeks for that visit to happen," says Kovacs. There should instead be trade mandates compelling "immediate" visits as soon as a crisis occurs.

Kovacs also urges a more aggressive public outreach to support legislation percolating in Congress to mandate that all food content be traceable. The Europeans have a similar model, and it works. Evolving legislation in the U.S. would also propose recall power for the FDA.

"The food industry must work publicly, and on the Hill, to strengthen the FDA's oversight and enforcement prerogatives," says Kovacs. "The more of a leadership role the industry can provide the FDA, the more of a leadership role as problem-solver it carves out for itself."

It is capital in the credibility bank for when the next tragic "rogue event" occurs, as it inevitably will.

(Continued from page 113)

Such groups live in anticipation of crisis. They merely needed to fill in the words "spinach," "E.coli," etc., on existing templates to launch their own information campaign the very day of the outbreak. Had it been a salmonella crisis, they would have typed in the word "chicken," propagating the same or similar messages worldwide. Reviewing media coverage from the summer of 2006 to the present, we see that "critics" of the industry are constantly quoted. There's a good chance that many of those unidentified critics are bloggers.

The spinach industry responded quickly. It held a press conference and chose the National Press Club in Washington, D.C. as the locale, thus maximizing media attention. Industry spokespeople also knew what to say. They did not explain soil test results or provide a mass of confusing detail, which would only have seeded distrust and confusion.

Instead, the industry described the steps it was taking to solve the problem as well as the steps it still intended to take. They stated what was known, and what still needed to be learned. They promised to continue reporting to the media when new information became available. Meanwhile, the industry had its own internal hotlines set up so that its spokespersons would be apprised of all new developments—from soil test results to further death and illness reports—at the soonest possible time.

Leaks were an obvious possibility and so was the spreading of dangerous misinformation. It was thus essential to set up a monitoring apparatus to review and analyze all pertinent blogs as well as print media.

WAR OF ATTRITION

Yet, the sample coverage above dramatizes that time was not on the side of the industry. Now begins the war of attrition—a war that the industry can, without question, win. We see, even in the context of the *Kansas City Star* article, how the industry is taking a leadership role and finding ways to collaborate with the government.

Based on the industry's overall performance since the crisis began, there is every reason to expect that the message of progress and the pursuit of a permanent solution will continue to be restated more forcefully in the future. Part of almost every crisis strategy is to respond at once to negative messages with credible positive ones. If reporters see the glass half-empty ("we still don't know how the contamination happened"), you come back at them with why the glass is actually half-full ("tracing the foodborne illness was an unprecedented breakthrough").

The industry has further underscored its leadership role with direct outreach to consumers. It has disseminated information on how to properly prepare spinach. Strong messages about the overall value of spinach in a well-balanced diet have also not been lost on its audiences. The trade associations played a key role at this point, proactively seeking media outlets to discuss future safeguards the organization is now pursuing.

As of this writing, spinach consumption is rising fast, reaching pre-crisis levels, despite the FDA's failure to identify the cause of the outbreak and the lingering possibility of a downtick in public confidence as a result. Again, though, it's a war of attrition. Polls have shown consumers still trusting the produce industry and still willing to eat spinach. Some crises are won or lost within weeks. Others require long-term, integrated campaigns that, as in this case, must leverage every positive future development to maximize public confidence.

In such crises, you need to be prepared to respond to the good news as well as the bad.

PHARMA: A CHRONIC CHALLENGE

The food industry is subject to a range of regulatory challenges and crises similar to what faces virtually every industry. It is not immune

(Continued on page 120)

The Fine Art of Product Recalls

For heavily regulated industries like food and Pharma, the product recall is a definitive crisis. It is an admission of failure in one specific area that can tarnish or even destroy the reputation of an entire company. The danger for Merck, for example, is that its entire corporate brand could become directly identified with a single product like Vioxx.

The corollary danger is that the fever could spread from product to product. For example, in the aftermath of the spinach crisis, lettuce, cauliflower, and lima beans were at risk as well. The industry knew it, and effectively implemented a strategy to prevent the collateral damage.

To be sure, we all learn from past example and the success of such recent recalls is based in large part on a careful study of what other industries and companies have done in similar circumstances. If not an exact science, a code of standards and best practices has evolved.

To begin with, five elements define a successful product recall:

✔ **Consumer protection.** The recall must be managed to prevent harm or further harm to the public. To achieve nationwide compliance, the logistics of a recall can rival a complex military operation.

✔ **Brand protection.** Brands are based on a promise and safety is usually an integral part of the promise. The recall must be managed to ensure confidence in the company's product line irrespective of the one bad apple. People do not now think "Ford" when they think "exploding engines." They think "Pinto."

✔ **Identifying opportunity.** Even in today's world, corporate reputations may actually improve after a responsible and well-explained product recall. If the company is being proactive, it is sending a message about its honesty and its concern.

✔ **Improving relationships with regulators.** Companies that handle recalls effectively create a fund of goodwill among the involved agencies that could serve them in very good stead in the long term, after the recall itself is forgotten.

✔ **Business recovery.** At the end of the day, the top line should still be strong and, ideally, unaffected.

These stakes speak to corporate viability at the most fundamental levels. Any company that manufactures a product that could ever conceivably be recalled must therefore plan well in advance for a recall that, hopefully, will never happen. The plan cannot and should not be written in stone, but the resources must be in readiness. Corporate spokespersons should be trained and rehearsed on a very regular basis.

The first step is a product recall action template. The template will vary from situation to situation, but these ten action points are a practicable beginning:

1. *Meet with the decision-making team* (executive/leadership, communication, technical expert). Within less than two hours, determine known information, what more will be coming in, and what can be said based on what you know now.

2. *Activate the plan* based on careful assessment of the situation and the expected demands for information by the public, media, and shareholders.

3. Bring in *needed resources* (human, technical, and mechanical supplies as specified in your pre-planning activities). Activate added personnel and consultants or agencies.

4. Bring together a *communication team*; brief them on the event, advise on what can be communicated now, and delegate assignments.

5. *Meet with upper management* to advise on current ac-

tivities and when you can anticipate releasing information in accordance with the organization's role in the response.

6. Make *telephone contact with the governmental agencies* involved to learn what communication they are planning, Coordinate timing for the release of information.

7. Line up your *spokespersons* or get ready to be the spokesperson. Let spokespersons know that you will need them available to the media, and that you want to brief them on the messages prior to their speaking with media. Let them know what background material on the event you can provide to update them, and when they can expect it.

8. *Prepare your message development team.* Personally review and approve materials yourself for release.

9. Determine a time frame for full crisis team meetings to *reassess the situation.* Every crisis is different, but it's likely that, for a product recall, the full team should be reconvening at no more than six-hour intervals during the first couple of days and no more than twelve-hour intervals after that and for the duration of the crisis.

10. Make certain to *fully communicate and update* your staff, board, decision-making team, and partners several times during the first 48 hours and beyond that as may be needed.

(Continued from page 117)

to accounting scandals or employment discrimination lawsuits. That said, their challenge tends to be more acute than chronic. Typical crises involve foodstuffs that, when ingested, cause harm. The consequences can be awful on a massive scale, but they don't happen every day.

By contrast, the pharmaceutical industry faces a *chronic* problem because the controversies are matters of 24/7 debate, and because there are so many different, equally threatening controversies going on at the same time.

Among numerous other areas of controversy, consider that, on any given day, a single pharmaceutical company may have to deal with public and media interest in:

- Major product safety litigation;
- FDA approval process;
- direct-to-consumer advertising;
- generic drug availability;
- reimportation;
- off-label uses; and
- patent disputes involving developing nations.

Each of these areas obviously merits exhaustive issue analysis and strategic treatment. For this modest review, our intent is to simply underscore some of the challenges involved and suggest where general solutions might lie.

Major product litigation. If today there is a dominant model for how pharmaceutical companies strategize product cases, it's fair to say that Bayer pioneered that model in the early years of this century when it faced multiple lawsuits over the now-withdrawn cholesterol drug Baycol.

Bayer quickly settled cases filed by claimants whom the company agreed had actually been harmed, but served notice that it would aggressively defend against all other lawsuits (the vast majority). After winning its first major trial in Texas, Bayer's litigation strategy became the centerpiece of its overall communications strategy, and the combined effort bore fruit when *The Wall Street Journal* ran feature coverage.

Not just meant as a deterrent to frivolous cases, such litigation-based communications campaigns are also brand-protection

(Continued on page 123)

Issues Management: Asked and Answered

Among the components of grassroots issues campaigns itemized in Chapter 8, we included surveys and polls that can either reinforce broad support for your position or disclose ongoing or incipient vulnerabilities. Strategically, an objective survey can encourage you to proceed in your aggressive advocacy of a particular position or it can take you back to the proverbial drawing board.

When, for example, Cox Communications launched "Take Charge!"—its award-winning program to educate parents and kids on how to control television and online content in their homes—the company's national poll found an overwhelming majority of adults very concerned about the content their children view and that they were aware of parental controls, but that they simply did not know how to use those controls.

Action: Cox included usage guidance as a key part of the "Take Charge" agenda.

Tactically, polling can provide empirical support to influence what the media reports and how they report it.

When, for example, the spinach industry grappled with a nationwide recall, it hired a pollster to assess public confidence. 63% of respondents were "very confident" or "somewhat confident" of the industry's ability to fix the problem. 52% percent said they would buy spinach within three months of the FDA signing off on a bill of health. In fact, 17% of those respondents said they would do so "right away."

Action: The industry was able to deliver the very powerful message that "consumers are shaken, but are confident in spinach growers' steps to ensure safety."

In communications, nothing works better than the support of disinterested third parties. When that support represents a sizable majority of end users, it creates a trend. Journalists don't have to take your word for it. They can simply report what over 60% of America thinks about spinach!

(Continued from page 121)

communications campaigns. By publicizing its resolve to withstand pressures from the plaintiffs' bar, Bayer was powerfully affirming a pride in its own corporate brand and underscoring self-confidence in its corporate good citizenship.

To a great extent, Merck's strategy with respect to Vioxx mirrors this antecedent. However, much more than with Baycol, the volume and intensity of media interest and scrutiny has been ratcheted up as a result of Merck's decision to try each Vioxx lawsuit independently. From a communications standpoint, we were suddenly talking not about the management of one big centralized informational campaign, but many separate ones in separate regional as well as national media markets.

If the Vioxx trials prove anything, it's that the outcome of every pharmaceutical case is up for grabs. The defense wins one, the plaintiff wins another. As the headlines swing back and forth on a daily basis, public opinion is also up for grabs. Investor relations are likewise in constant play and, with it, the value of pharmaceutical stocks.

Right now lawyers and communications professionals are presumably urging the same advice on their pharmaceutical clients. What drug on your list might be the next Vioxx? Identify it now. Review its entire history from the earliest R&D to the marketing plan, and from FDA approval to current advertising.

FDA approval. One day pharmaceutical companies must face contentious regulators. The next day they're accused by NGOs of being in cahoots with those very same regulators. The regulatory "dance" we noted in our discussion of the food industry is all the more nuanced as a result. Companies and regulators must create some distance from each other to affirm the integrity of the process. Both sides need to set mutual expectations with a keen eye to public opinion.

More than other regulatory agencies, the FDA is itself exposed to immense public criticism. If you Google "FDA approval controversies," the links go on for page after page, mostly regurgitating bitter discussions among authoritative sources about drugs already approved. In each instance, the manufacturers are naturally exposed too as it's their products that are under siege. (The FDA simultaneously faces withering criticism for not approving drugs that dying patients want as a last resort.)

It's doubtful that any clear picture of the approval process would significantly stem the criticisms. Yet such explications should still be part of the industry's defensive ammunition. If an approved drug is under attack, a simple powerful description of why it passed regulatory muster is part of the messaging.

Direct to consumer advertising. The more effectively Big Pharma advertises, the more it leads with its chin. As one blogger wrote, "it's hard to tell the difference between pharmaceutical commercials and car commercials." Competitive pressures presumably demand slick ads, but the slicker the ad, the more outraged the response by some health watchdogs and consumer advocates. In turn, pressures by these critics may lead to renewed regulatory oversight. As of this writing, for example, lawmakers have asked Amgen and Johnson & Johnson to suspend all consumer advertising of their anemia medications until U.S. regulators do an *additional* safety review.

The blog quoted above—it's the health channel of *newstarget. com*—features well over 100 experts, including doctors testifying to the evils of direct-to-consumer advertising. Among their many recurrent themes, the new drugs being hyped offer no real improvement over what's already on the market. Doctors are, they say, being seduced as well. Over and over, lax oversight by the FDA is blamed for this "self-medicating society," which raises an ever-present possibility that the regulators will react strongly and start controlling ad content more aggressively.

Big Pharma has not apparently taken this bull by the proverbial horns. It's a delicate balance in any event. Too much back-and-forth public debate might further highlight the issue to the industry's disadvantage. That said, it would seem that stronger position papers will at least balance the other side's unremitting attack.

Generic drugs. Public awareness of generic drug availability poses a constant challenge to the reputation of drug manufacturers. They must always be defending the fact that they're in business to make money.

Image ads showing the human benefits of pharmaceutical R&D are all to the good. At the same time, the industry really has no choice but to explicitly and aggressively remind the world—perhaps even in the context of its image ads—that profits drive research. Message: What is the alternative? Follow-up message: Would the public prefer socialized medicine?

Prescription drug pricing. Here, too, the industry can educate the public on how profits drive research. There's an additional wrinkle, which is the inevitable question, "How much profit is enough profit?" Cases abound of pharmaceutical companies nailed for making too much. In 2007, for example, the state of Hawaii reached a $1.15 million settlement with Dey Inc., which manufactures respiratory drugs (including Albuterol), and which reportedly inflated prices 800%.

Reimportation. The dynamics are similar to generic drugs since the issue is cheaper availability across the border. The difference is that these drugs are exported prescription medicines. From a PR standpoint, the issue is exacerbated because senior citizens are frequently in the news for riding buses to Canada to buy prescriptions at a fraction of what they cost back home.

Here, the most powerful communications weapon in the industry's arsenal could be the safety question as these seniors could be buying counterfeit medications.

Off-label uses. On this issue, which involves the prescribing of drugs for treatment not specified on the label, the pharmaceutical industry is fairly conspicuous in its own defense and has rallied many expert supporters. At the same time, the industry's legal defeats have fueled industry opponents. A watershed event occurred in May

2004 when Pfizer pleaded guilty to illegally marketing Neurontin for unapproved use and settled with the Department of Justice. The price tag was $430 million, the second-largest settlement ever in a healthcare fraud prosecution.

Off-label uses crystallize many issues described above. Liabilities are uncovered that might not have otherwise become causes of action: The charge, for example, that Neurontin poses a high suicide risk (which plaintiffs and NGOs say the FDA knew about all along). Off-labeling also provides industry opponents additional opportunity to win points on corporate greed and castigate industry marketing practices.

It's particularly germane that off-labeling further complicates the relationship between the industry and the regulators. As Randall Stafford, a professor of medicine at Stanford University, put it, "both physicians and patients have misunderstood the role of the FDA. I think there's sort of a presumption that if a drug has made it onto the market, the FDA has vouched for its safety and efficacy for all of its potential uses." To be sure, the most controversial and damaging drug lawsuits of the last few decades have involved FDA-approved products.

Message: Pharmaceutical companies are never home safe. They must be ready to do battle in courts of law and in the court of public opinion long after their dance with the government is over.

Patent disputes involving developing nations. John Iwanicki, a partner at Banner & Witcoff, a leading intellectual property law firm, expresses it very well. "I know of no more agonizing decision than what pharmaceutical companies face when their vital business interests require them to protect patents on life-saving drugs in poorer nations. It is a very good example of why companies in crisis must have the benefit of multidisciplinary advisors. They need variegated counsel to address their variegated concerns."

Predictably, companies trying to protect patents in Third World nations (or in even more developed nations like Brazil) are depicted by NGOs and some reporters as heartless, inhumane, profit-obsessed, etc. Those perceptions are hardly discouraged by instances of faith-based shareholder groups taking their own companies to task for such hard-line positions. At the same time, the settlements that have been brokered for broader distribution of drugs to treat AIDS and Avian Flu become all the more crucial as they are opportunities to recast the debate so that corporations look like problem-solvers rather than obstacles to humanitarian progress.

The larger communications challenge is to also go beyond such specific issues and propagate a more generalized counter-story that might…

- ✔ Convey community commitment. For example, The Partnership for Prescription Assistance campaign, which includes many Big Pharma participants, features a "Help is Here Express" promo in which two buses crisscross the country, stopping off in hundreds of communities to educate the uninsured and under-insured about drug assistance programs.

- ✔ Use third-party endorsements with broad popular appeal. For example, as of this writing, television celebrity Montel Williams is the spokesperson for The Partnership for Prescription Assistance.

- ✔ Engage in comprehensive communications efforts to promote healthy diets and exercise routines. Such campaigns simultaneously talk about the industry's extensive R&D activities.

- ✔ Help the public understand the economics of the pharmaceutical business. The message needs to be delivered in the most straightforward terms: It takes 10 to 15 years to create a drug, and it costs billions of dollars to research, manufacture, and market our products even as we navigate the FDA's labyrinthine approval process. Proudly disseminate the corollary message that profits allow production of life-saving drugs. Take away those profits, and there will be nothing to infringe.

The salient challenge for pharmaceutical companies is that their business interests are perceived as in direct opposition to public safety. Even alleged polluters do not face quite such a challenge. It is widely assumed (and often correctly) that the cost of discharging environmentally harmless wastes may hurt in the short term, but will not savage the corporate bottom line and, in the long run, may actually enhance it.

At the same time, identifying and tailoring messages for specific audiences is possibly more important for Pharma than other industries. In part, that's because the challenge is so chronic and so many different audiences are affected. Among those audiences, investors and analysts must see sound business practices in place. They must be reassured that, for example, compromises with foreign governments do not expose the corporation to all-out global infringement. They must also be reassured that projected bottom-line losses will be amply compensated by accelerated gains elsewhere.

The need to balance those reassurances with believable commitment to fair and cost-efficient product delivery defines the pharmaceutical industry's formidable communications task in the years and decades ahead.

It may be worth mentioning by way of conclusion that it was, of course, the pharmaceutical industry that set the standard for all crisis management during the Tylenol tampering case of 25 years ago. Len Biegel, one of the communications consultants who advised Johnson & Johnson during the crisis, reminds us (in his book *Never Say Never*, published in 2007 by Bricktower Press) that that company was guided throughout the ordeal by its own credo, which begins with the following words...

"We believe our first responsibility is to the doctors, nurses and patients, to mothers and fathers and all others who use our products and services."

So Don't Forget...

The Regulatory Dance...

- During any regulatory investigation, the moment of truth happens when you decide to stay on defense or go on the offense.

- In a defense strategy, the objective is to establish the strongest possible cooperation with the agency, which could even include joint press releases. An offense strategy should always carry the fight beyond issues related to your company. The best counter-attack is based on larger themes of fairness, due process, and the damages that the government's action causes.

Food Crises...

- Information flow is critical. The media and the public need to be certain that, as soon as you can be helpful, you will directly communicate all crisis-related developments. Speed is of the essence—you need to immediately communicate what you know and what you are doing to find out more.

- Become part of the solution. Publicly lobby for reinvigorated standards and enforcement. Transform crisis into opportunity by disseminating safety information and discussing future safeguards. Think long-term and your audiences will too.

The Pharma Wars...

- Industry crises are constant and multifarious, involving diverse audiences with opposing interests. Tailor each campaign to specific audiences.

- Your interests are perceived to conflict with public welfare. Tell the counter story. Show the human side of what you accomplish. Recruit popular public figures as advocates. Embrace the profit motive. Show why the success of your business saves lives and jobs.

TEN

The Family Jewels: Media Strategies in Product Liability Crises

There's a reason why major product cases can generate more media attention, with more serious consequence, than just about any other species of litigation, including the front-page corporate scandals like those that rocked the world in the summer of 2002. Those scandals will continue to fuel news columns for months and years to come, but not everyone in the world worked for Enron or Andersen or WorldCom or lived in communities decisively affected by the malfeasance.

On the other hand, if a Tylenol bottle is poisoned, if a Pinto blows up, if an airplane manufacturer sells faulty parts, anyone anywhere can be affected at any time. That sells newspapers.

Companies deal generally with two types of product liability cases that usually require contrasting PR strategies. In the first type, the goal is to keep the product's reputation intact or to even improve its reputation—to fend off, both in a court of law and in the media, any imputation that the product is defective or dangerous.

In the second type, the product has become indefensible. It's either off the market or will be soon. Often, as with asbestos, the company is immersed in mass tort litigation and fundamentally different rules therefore pertain. Even the general rule of never saying "no comment," or always returning a reporter's phone call, might no longer apply.

Media and crisis management are equal parts art and science. Even the basic rules are made to be broken.

PRESERVING MARKETPLACE INTEGRITY

Let's look first at product liability cases where the clear goal is to defend the product and ensure continued marketplace viability.

Develop a theme

Once the lawsuit is filed, the first task is the most important one: Develop a theme. This theme is essentially the same message for the press as for the jury, although, for the jury, the theme usually gets presented in both long and short form.

The long form encompasses a myriad of supporting facts, including technical facts, rendered in language easily comprehensible to the laity. The short form is the bare message itself minus accompanying detail. It is usually repeated in court, before and during summation, to ensure the jury gets the message in its unmistakable essence.

That short form is the one to use with the media. Sometimes the trade press will want more elaborate material if, for instance, it's an automotive publication read by industry professionals conversant with the specific workings of an internal combustion engine. Generally, though, the evening news wants only a reasoned assertion that the product is a sound one.

The theme is the final distilled result of intense reading, knowledge of the product's history, numerous conversations with the people who developed the product, and an intimate familiarity with how the product is marketed. The delivery of the theme by a company spokesperson is all the more credible and powerful as a result of such informed comprehension.

Anne Kimball, a partner at Chicago's Wildman Harrold, who has represented the gun, alcohol, food and pharmaceutical industries, among others, offers a typical "theme" in a case involving the involuntary discharge of a firearm:

The gun is built to discharge only when the trigger is pulled, and there is no possible way anyone can demonstrate that it discharges under any other circumstance. Mr. Jones may not have wanted to pull the trigger, but pull it he did. It's unfortunate, but there is no other possible explanation.

"Themes" are not quite the same as the "message points" discussed in Chapter 5. Message points are effective in dealing with the press but they may not be exculpatory. In the Catholic Church crisis, for example, the message points might suggest the potential innocence of the accused but go on to declare that, if there is evidence of misconduct, the Church will cooperate with civil authorities to the fullest extent.

The theme in a product liability case includes no such promise. It is an unqualified assertion that the product belongs on the market. It wins acquittals in courts of law and in the Court of Public Opinion.

Restrict the battlefield

Justice, however, is not really blind. Themes in product liability cases are subject to intervening variables. Since these cases affect the welfare of every voter in the country, they are often filed with political motives resolutely in tow.

Jurors, conditioned by their own political sensibilities, often ignore irrefutable facts supporting the defense theme. How much more so the millions of consumers who are not charged by a judge or obliged to follow any rules in making their determinations about the safety of a product!

For the gun industry, for example, politics and product liability are linked inextricably. NRA hardball has further politicized these cases for many citizens. If gun control advocates can't beat the lobbyists in the legislatures, they will do so in court.

(Continued on page 139)

The Latest Pandemic: Data Security Breaches in an Age of High Anxiety

Not long after the first edition of this book was published in 2004, one of the nation's largest data brokers, ChoicePoint, discovered that it had been duped into providing records containing personal data to an organized crime ring that had falsely registered as a small business ChoicePoint client. Not long afterward, in February 2005, the world learned that the personal data of 163,000 citizens had been handed over to this criminal organization.

Eventually, it was also revealed that a similar data breach at ChoicePoint had occurred in 2002. The 2002 incident was smaller, but certainly not insignificant, as it involved around $1 million in fraud. Among the many problems that have since confronted ChoicePoint is the lingering question of why that earlier incident did not prompt the company to install better safeguards against such breaches. The fact patterns were certainly close enough. In both cases, bogus businesses had been set up for soliciting names and social security numbers from ChoicePoint data. In both cases, even the national identity (Nigerian) of the culprits was the same.

If there was a good reason why history had repeated itself so unpleasantly, the public never really heard it.

ChoicePoint is a data aggregation company based in Georgia that acts as a private intelligence service to government and industry. The company maintains over 17 billion records of individuals and businesses, which it sells to an estimated 100,000 clients. From a crisis management standpoint, one of the daunting problems in dealing with breaches is that they typically involve just such companies, along with credit agencies, banks, and—as the 2006 Veterans Administration breach proved—government offices. In other words, the germ has infected our systems at the very point where our systems need to be perceptibly impregnable.

Notwithstanding the earlier breach at ChoicePoint, 2005 resonates as a watershed year. Before then, crisis and communications managers dealt with "hard" product liability areas: Cars, guns, asbestos, etc. Of course those liabilities are still chronic and acute but, after 2005, another genus of liability was roiling public anxiety. *CSO* magazine calls it the "unbearable lightness of data."

So far, the loss to U.S. businesses and consumers represented by data theft in all its forms is equivalent to the GNP of an oil-rich Middle Eastern nation: $56.6 billion in 2005. More than one in four Americans had digital data exposed between 2005 and 2006, and more than three of every four companies in a recent survey said they had been exposed to a security breach by fraudsters, up from about one in four companies per year earlier. "Unbearable" indeed!

The astounding number of data breaches since early 2005 confirms data security as a significant new staple of the crisis manager's craft. As of August, 2007, a chronology of breaches compiled by Privacy Rights Clearinghouse includes over 700 separate incidents compromising around 160 million separate records since January 1, 2005. Private and state universities loom large on the Privacy Rights Clearinghouse list but so too do government agencies, banks, and accounting firms. Ernst &Young appears three times. Boeing makes the list. So does IBM.

ChoicePoint is worth a closer look for both its mistakes and successes since its security problems began. We've already noted the apparent failure to explain why the October 2004 incident could happen after such a similar event in 2002. In the aftermath of this second breach, ChoicePoint notified police but did not notify the individuals affected until February 2005. Even then, the company only notified California residents, which it was required to do by state law. Not until a public outcry arose, and a Congressional rebuke followed on, did the company reach agreement with twenty or so state attorneys general to contactan additional 128,000 people. Ultimately, the company was forced to pay a $10 million fine to the FTC and agree to another $5 million to compensate victims.

Lesson: Full disclosure and direct contact with victims are among the fundamental first steps in managing a data security breach. Those steps have now become standard crisis management practice, perhaps as a direct result of the lessons learned from ChoicePoint's failure to fully and voluntarily respond at the get-go.

As late as March of 2005, ChoicePoint was still tentative in its public communications strategy. That month, *CSO*—a high-authority online publication written for security executives—requested an interview with ChoicePoint's Chief Information Security Officer, Rich Baich. As *CSO* later reported (May 2005), "Sounding upbeat, he said that he was trying to convince his public relations department to let him set the record straight. 'They need to let this happen,' he said. 'Look, I'm the Chief Information Security Officer. Fraud doesn't relate to me.' He indicated that he would be doing the CISO community a service by explaining to the media why fraud was not an information security issue."

ChoicePoint later denied his request to grant the interview. It was a false start but not a fatal one. The outreach engine finally cranked up and aggressive and persistent messages were disseminated, focusing on what ChoicePoint was doing to remediate this global problem. The company initiated dialogue with numerous privacy experts and academics. Online posts by the firm were straightforward and seemingly transparent, marshaling evidence of the specific correctives that were being undertaken.

By September 2006, a Gartner Group report was asserting that "ChoicePoint has now become a role model for protecting customer data privacy." Particularly impressive, Sen. Charles Schumer told *The New York Times* that, "I was worried that a fine would be seen as the cost of doing business… But I have to say, ChoicePoint has become a model company." One might have expected that activist New York Democrat to remain skeptical. Instead, his endorsement spoke volumes on behalf of ChoicePoint.

The fact that ChoicePoint, too, had been victimized by the scammers was another strong asset on the communications front. Third-party villains are always serviceable in managing a crisis and nowhere more so than with data breaches. Jody Westby offers a pointed comparison. The public expects the CIA and FBI to function competently and securely, "but people are also aware and accepting of the fact that there will be rogue agents like Aldrich Ames and Robert Hansen and that those rogue agents will do significant damage," says Westby, the CEO of Global Cyber Risk LLC, which provides advisory and legal services in areas such as cyber security, privacy, cybercrime, and infrastructure protection to corporations and governments in the U.S., Europe, and developing countries.

"Even with the highest, most critical security concerns, there's the expectation of periodic breakdowns—which is tolerable, provided the proper policies and procedures are in place and it involves a bad actor whose deeds can finally be isolated and stopped," adds Westby.

The casting of the villain in the ChoicePoint crisis was all the more effective because it was done so matter-of-factly as part of the company's informational outreach. It just seemed to be a given that nefarious outside parties were at the heart of the matter. As some of ChoicePoint's detractors continued to point out, however, there was no hacker involved in this breach, nor even a thief who walked off with a computer. ChoicePoint itself sold the data to the bad guys—with no intention of harm, to be sure, yet failing to provide itself with the same oversight that it is in business to provide others. No matter: The third-party villain motif was handled artfully enough to overshadow the "shoemaker's kids have no shoes" motif.

If imperfect, ChoicePoint's experience is additionally instructive because it shows that serious missteps, even in so critical an area, are not necessarily irreversible. In some ways, ChoicePoint was the testing ground for future data crisis management and communications. As a result, we are now able to more clearly define what should be done and what should not be done in such situations.

Just three years ago, data breaches represented an untamed frontier of crisis communications. Today, the fundamental elements are being refined to include...

- A *promise* to protect customers' personal data along with a credible sense of how that is going to be done;

- a palpable and believable expression of *concern* about customer welfare;

- a visible enterprise security program that links privacy and security and involves oversight, controls, annual reviews, and updates; and

- convincing evidence that the company is *learning fast* from past mistakes, and will incorporate what it learns into future efforts.

Tactical best practices have likewise been implemented...

- Plan a media strategy through websites and blogs. Anticipate the data exposure problems that may likely occur in the future and create a "dark site" now, which will be ready to go "live" as soon as a crisis occurs.

- Identify those in the blogging, academic, legal, NGO, and government communities who are likely to be sympathetic and helpful. By doing so, companies can populate their own and other online resources with rich content from supportive third-party spokespersons.

- Train or outsource a data exposure hotline team that can handle the communications, legal, and policy issues. Outsourcing provides an adjustable and coordinated capacity to manage issues and meet call volumes without major investments.

- Consider self-reporting and even apologizing to the public. It will show that the company is one of the good actors and will thus dramatically lessen how long a story stays in the news. However, the messaging here needs to be fairly nuanced. It could seem contradictory to apologize for a situation and claim to be a victim at the same time.

- Get buy-in now from professional and trade associations. Again it will show that the company is part of the solution, not the problem. Map out an agenda of collaborative efforts with respect to both any current situation as well as longer-range public awareness campaigns.

Experts say the security theft problem will grow by a factor of 20 before the decade is ended. Meanwhile, observers like Jody Westby question the commitment of some big businesses to solve the problem if doing so requires executive and board time for oversight and expenditures to support an enterprise security program. Early court and administrative decisions lean toward an understanding that security cannot be 100%, but a company is expected to have the right policies, processes, and procedures in place to prevent, mitigate, and respond to security breaches.

In this regard, crisis management must be collaborative, it must be transparent, it must be proactive, and it must be part of the company's security program rather than an ad hoc exercise after an event. The alternative is recurrent and increasingly serious systemic breakdowns that will continue to feed organized crime, cyber terrorists, and bad actors—including insiders.

(Continued from page 133)

In the last decade, Kimball has been defending a spate of cases filed by municipalities against her firearms industry clients. She's won most of them, and she's done so by relying on a second, supporting "theme:"

A court of law is not the place to determine who should and should not have access to firearms. The regulation of the firearms industry is a matter for you, as citizens, to take up with your representatives in Congress or your local legislatures. The integrity of our judicial system depends on your not confusing the issues. The issue here is simply whether or not the gun exploded, all by itself, in Mr. Jones' face.

It's much tougher to de-politicize politically charged cases in the press than in court. "It depends on the journalist," says Kimball. "Sometimes they're listening to you, sometimes they're not." But you should still explicitly remind reporters that your case is one issue and that the law of the land is another.

Different products create different issues in our politically correct and sensitive society, whether the products are SUVs, fatty foodstuffs, or supplements taken by athletes. Again and again, Kimball must argue for separation of powers. She must point out that politically motivated plaintiffs ought to be taking their cases to Congress and, if Congress wants to further regulate how certain products are marketed, it is free to do so. In the gun litigation, she began making that point to the media early on, in anticipation of their fervid interest in these cases.

There are thus two strategic imperatives for the defense in many product cases. First, affirm the safety of the product. Second, keep the discussion as disinterested as possible, in and out of the courtroom.

Fine-tune the themes

Defense themes vary from industry to industry. For companies in the alcohol industry, the typical theme developed by litigators like Kimball emphasizes numbers:

Alcohol is responsibly consumed by millions of Americans every day. Those who abuse it represent a small minority and should be helped. The alcohol industry is heavily regulated and has responded to initiatives to minimize the damage its product can cause. There is no just reason to fault the industry for the problems of a small number of abusers, especially in light of industry initiatives to encourage responsible consumption.

The theme plays well, mainly because the public already believes it. Alcohol manufacturers and distributors have indeed been historically amenable to regulation, while a significant percentage of the public does, in fact, drink responsibly every day. In Kimball's experience, alcohol industry clients are usually vindicated, legally and in the media, even in tragic drunk-driving cases.

For companies defending medical devices, Kimball describes a few themes to play for jurors and reporters:

- Acknowledge that most medical devices have attendant risk.

- Emphasize the fact that the government has approved the product. Unlike other products, "you already have a strong tribunal on your side when you defend medical devices," says Kimball. "People know the FDA and people instinctively trust it." (As we saw in Chapter 9, however, FDA approval won't necessarily exculpate some products either legally or publicly.)

- Underscore the positive health benefits of the product.

Once the themes are developed, espouse them aggressively. "Plaintiffs' lawyers are getting their messages to reporters well before they file suit, and they often hang out in the same bars the reporters do," says Kimball. "So you've got to act fast. It's got to be part of the initial case strategy."

PRESERVING A DELICATE BALANCE

If you happen to be a company with a name like Owens Corning, forget most of what you've just learned.

Mass tort litigation invariably presents a different public relations burden. In this species of product litigation, liability has often already been established. Now the issue is: How much liability? Also, there are often thousands of cases filed against your company, often with different legal counsel handling different cases in different jurisdictions.

Curb thy tongue

In mass tort litigation, "any comments you make about your case can directly affect every other case of the same nature that involves the company in ways that can be extremely damaging," advises Mark Goodman, a partner at Debevoise & Plimpton in New York.

So you don't just trot out a few message points and deliver them at will. Often, the best thing to say, even after you've won a case, is "no comment."

Example: In July, you win a case that's part of a mass tort litigation and you crow about it to the press. In August, your company loses the same kind of case, with the same claims and the same fact pattern, in a different jurisdiction. Now the jury retires to decide on punitives.

As Goodman points out, the plaintiff can then show your earlier press statements to the jurors for their consideration. Your gleeful expostulation sounds to them like gloating. You seem so pleased to be evading responsibility, to be getting away with murder.

The jurors aren't going to let you get away with it this time. They'll right the wrong by tacking on an extra $50 million or so in punitive damages.

Without seasoned legal and public relations counsel, it can get even worse.

Goodman, who has represented clients like Owens Corning in a variety of mass tort cases, offers another very bad case scenario. Assume all you do is to innocently inform the press that a case you litigated just settled for a mere $25,000. Considering the exposure in the case, that would seem a result you'd want the media to trumpet at full blast.

Yet that simple disclosure can "implicate your accounting procedures," as Goodman puts it, actually devaluing the company itself even as it attracts unwanted SEC scrutiny. Corporations must report reserve funds for contingency liability and they use a dollar amount average to calculate what they report. That average may be based on a combination of very high numbers and very low ones.

When you tell the press that a case settled for $25,000, the analysts will do a little simple arithmetic using $25,000 as a basis for evaluating the entire reserve. The company may, in fact, be sufficiently reserved, but the one settlement figure you disclosed befuddles subsequent calculations and creates a perception of under-funding.

Results: Stock values plummet and the regulators come knocking at your door. Now it's not just a question of paying more. It's a question of suddenly being worth much less.

Craft the message

In a gun case or a medical device case, the goal may be to keep the product viable. An aggressive media campaign serves that purpose. By contrast, in a mass tort product case, the first task at hand is to mandate vows of silence among all corporate spokespersons and to fashion a PR campaign that supports a sound legal strategy.

What should that PR campaign look like? What message point or theme can the media mavens roll out on behalf of a company that may be in bankruptcy, that is still litigating thousands of lawsuits, and that has been judged liable for manufacturing and marketing a deadly product a quarter of a century ago?

Goodman, using asbestos as an example, articulates a message point acknowledging some liability:

We are not defending the conduct of the company in the past, and we are not trying to minimize the damages suffered by claimants. We will compensate everyone who has suffered asbestos-related damages as a result of our business activities. But we will also fight hard legally to ensure that we are not held responsible for false claims, for damages that are not asbestos-related, or for damages unrelated to the manufacturing and marketing of asbestos by this company.

(Continued on page 146)

Establishing Privilege—and Keeping It

As communications professionals play ever greater roles formulating and implementing strategy and case management during litigation, an abiding problem vexes lawyers and their clients. "Litigation PR" is not in and of itself privileged. There is risk that a communications advisor will deliver critical advice, or be privy to extremely sensitive case-related information, that opponents can discover, disclose, and use to their advantage.

Fortunately, the problem is not insoluble.

Michael N. Levy, who heads the White Collar/Investigations and Enforcement group at the law firm McKee Nelson LLP in Washington, D.C., has provided comprehensive analysis of existing case law pertaining to privilege that puts the evolving issue in context.

As Levy shows, there is, in fact, substantial case law to support the position that information shared with non-attorney communications advisors is protected. The landmark case (involving an accountant) is *United States v. Kovel,* 296 F.2d 918 (2nd Cir. 1961), which held that, to maintain privilege, "the communication [must] be made in confidence for the purpose of obtaining legal advice from the lawyer. If what is sought is not legal advice but only accounting service...or if the advice sought is the accountant's rather than the lawyer's, no privilege exists."

Kovel used the analogy of a "translator" in that "[a]ccounting concepts are a foreign language to some lawyers in almost all cases, and to almost all lawyers in some cases." Since the lawyer's counsel is privileged and the "translations" are necessary for advising the client, the translations should be privileged as well.

Levy points out, however, that other rulings cut in different directions. *United States v. Adlman,* 68 F.3d 1495 (2nd Cir. 1995) did not distinguish an accounting firm's litigation-related work from other non-litigation work that an accounting firm provided the client. The court particularly noted that the firm's invoices did not distinguish litigation and non-litigation services. Yet, *In re Grand Jury Subpoenas,* 265 F. Supp. 2d 321 (S.D.N.Y. 2003) ruled that the attorney would be "undermined seriously" absent professional advice on the effects of public statements.

These mixed rulings suggest that the issue of privilege will ultimately be determined by *how* the relationship with non-attorney advisors is structured and implemented. The goal is to establish, in adherence to *Kovel*, that communications with PR counsel were made in confidence as an inextricable part of a process to obtain legal advice from lawyers.

Levy defines nine practical steps to reach that goal:

✔ The communications firm should preferably be one that specializes in litigation PR.

✔ The firm should be hired specifically to work on a particular litigation and not for traditional marketing/PR.

✔ The firm should be hired *early* in the legal process and hired as part of the legal team—rather than later, which would undercut any argument that the communications firm's counsel was a necessary component of the lawyer's privileged legal advice.

✔ If the firm is also doing other PR work for the client, a new contract should be drawn up just for the litigation work—a totally separate engagement with totally separate responsibilities.

✔ The lawyer should be hired first and the lawyer, not the client, should then hire the communications firm.

✔ Contract language should pointedly stipulate that the communications firm is retained as a facilitator, which substantively invokes *Kovel's* language ("translator") affirming privileged non-attorney counsel.

✔ All invoices billed by the communications firm should include direct reference to the facilitating/translating role.

✔ The lawyer should conduct all initial consultations involving
the client and the communications firm.

✔ The lawyer should be personally involved in all subsequent
client/PR firm communications or, failing that, the lawyer
should direct those communications.

The very fact that privilege is an issue of such concern underscores how critical public communications is perceived to
be during litigation and investigations. Some lawyers and clients
once needed to be convinced that PR counsel was at all important. Today they're taking careful steps to maximize its value.

(Continued from page 143)

Fashioned thus, the messaging avoids two pitfalls…

- The company is not commenting on behavior that dates back
two or three decades. As Goodman points out, that's a fight
the defendant won't likely win, especially in the press. Plaintiffs' attorneys can always find ways to cast aspersions on business decisions made so long ago in a dramatically different
business context. In the media, of course, reporters needn't
offer any real proof.

- The company is not trying to mitigate its liability by saying
that asbestos was universally thought to be a good product in
the past. True or not, the point simply won't wash in today's
media. The far better tack is to accept responsibility rather
than argue about ancient perceptions regarding a product that
turned out to be a bad one.

Having uttered the mea culpa for past actions and inactions,
the company can now complement contrition with a positive and
socially useful stated goal. Goodman's next message point:

It is essential that we protect ourselves from liability that is not ours because it is our goal to make sure that we have sufficient reserves to compensate everyone who is justly entitled to compensation from us. Only by challenging unjust liability can we guarantee a just outcome for the many people who have suffered in this situation.

The fact that 130 million people were actually exposed to asbestos, while 200 million people claimed to have been, supports the message on factual economic grounds. But such messaging also suggests the possibility of a public opinion swing. Stories that have been largely negative in the past can eventually present the company in a positive light.

For products that, unlike asbestos, are still marketable, such a turnaround should be an abiding objective of corporate crisis planning. After all, the corporate purpose is to sell the product. A mere acquittal in a court of law is a Pyrrhic victory if, despite the findings of a jury, the public still has vague misgivings.

In our next chapter, we will look at a peculiar species of product liability crisis management that requires separate consideration, as it's all about a war that's been raging for decades and may well rage on for decades to come—at least somewhere in the world.

HUMANIZE THE SPOKESPERSON

It would seem that any product defense starts off at a disadvantage on the PR front. At best, the company is in the unenviable position of having to show the world that a product essential to its business does not cause grievous injury or death. At worst, there is a widespread, if baseless, presumption of guilt. "Anyone defending a corporation these days is starting off at a disadvantage, in any kind of case," comments Anne Kimball. There's always been bias against powerful "impersonal" business interests. Post-Enron, the bias is proportionately harder and faster.

(Continued on page 151)

Don't Be an 'Entity:' Media Strategies for Class Actions

Class actions exponentially raise the ante in the high-stakes poker game. Class actions are, after all, quintessentially public lawsuits beginning, as they do, with sweeps of the general population by plaintiffs' firms trolling for class members. It's hard to keep something like that secret.

Plaintiffs' lawyers have an additional advantage in class actions. Because their clients are a *mass* group of ostensible victims, it's harder to discredit the alleged suffering. In an individual lawsuit, the defendant may counter the plaintiff's claim to the sympathies of jurors and the public. You can show contributory negligence. You may even be able to raise doubts about the character of the "victim."

But what if there are 10,000 claimants? Have they all contributed to their own injuries? Are they all of dubious character? Class actions generate widespread perception of a whole human population suffering at the hands of an indifferent entity. That entity is your company—and your exculpatory options are diminished 10,000-fold. Merck might have had good legal reasons to fight the Vioxx wars on a case-by-case basis, but the company gained some advantage on the communications front as well, simply because it's been able to target individual plaintiffs and vitiate their individual claims.

(As this book was going into production, Merck announced that it was prepared to pay $4.85 billion to settle almost 50,000 Vioxx lawsuits. By making this offer, Merck apparently abandoned its case-by-case strategy as a way to settle the entire controversy once and for all. As of this writing, 85% of qualified plaintiffs must still agree to the deal.)

By contrast, in class actions, companies require a more complex strategy. At the very least, it becomes all the more important for the defendants to affirm positive messages about themselves. From the inception of a class action, the first order of business is to *stop being an entity and become something more human.* If the company cannot minimize the sympathy for the other side, it can at least create sympathy for itself. Toward that end:

- ✔ **Show off your people**—your employees and customers. Merck is relevant in this context as well. As we discussed in Chapter 8, in 2006, the company ran television commercials showcasing the *human* benefits of the work that its *human* employees were doing. The content was not directly related to any litigation nor was the word "Vioxx" ever uttered. Yet these "image ads" exasperated the plaintiffs during one trial in New Orleans when a gag order precluded public discussion of the case. Only the defendant could speak to the public (and jury pool) because its communications were not case-related. The plaintiffs had no such institutional message of good tidings to convey. Such a strategy, used there for a single case, is pointedly effective for class actions as well.

- ✔ **Attack the messenger**—in other word's, the plaintiffs' lawyers, if appropriate, rather than the plaintiffs themselves. It's the opposite strategy from the typical approach in individual cases. In individual cases, the defendant doesn't attack plaintiff's counsel (barring some specific reason to do so). Even if the plaintiff's lawyer can be legitimately attacked, it won't necessarily diminish sympathy for his or her client. In class actions, on the other hand, there are tried-and-true ways to target opposing counsel. For example, the fact that plaintiffs' counsel stand to make millions while class members may see only a few dollars at day's end creates opportunity to seize on the public's perennial distrust of lawyers. In securities class actions, this strategy is all the more promising because the injuries are complex, the fact patterns difficult to understand, and the suffering less visual than, say, in product liability cases.

✔ **Talk about the future**—what the company is doing to remedy the very problems that prompted the class action. The goal is to establish leadership by jumping on the other side of the issue as a problem solver. Partnerships with public interest groups are naturally helpful here as they impart a palpable sense that the company isn't just talking about making things better, but establishing the kind of relationships that turn talk into action.

The best practices that govern not just the content, but the process of public communications during litigation, are likewise all the more exigent during class actions. For example:

✔ Don't speak though a "legal mouthpiece," but select and train spokespersons who show the company's human face. Supportive third parties who can talk about the issues driving the case are likewise invaluable.

✔ Use every milestone in the case—every motion, every ruling—as a possible pretext to reinforce your position. At the very least, expect plaintiffs' counsel to reach out to the media at such times and carefully monitor that outreach. It's how they keep the story alive. The newswires are particularly important at these junctures since they tend to run "process stories" (e.g.,"The jury was selected today in the case of...."). The wires also feed national and local newspapers everywhere.

✔ Blogs are especially powerful during class actions, both as opinion forums and as repositories of information. Expect plaintiffs to post their own blogs and recruit third-party supporters to post others. Monitor them carefully and, where appropriate, match them blog for blog.

✔ Daunting as they are from a communications standpoint, class actions do allow defendants one strategic advantage—time. Plaintiffs' firms must recruit before they can file. While their solicitations unfortunately ensure widespread public visibility, the public notices also mean that you can begin planning a public response well in advance. An ad in the newspaper soliciting your customers or clients, or those of other companies in your industry, is an obvious cue to set up a team and start coming up with a plan.

(Continued from page 147)

The strategic response is a veritable best practice for all product liability crises—humanize the corporation! That means…

- For court appearances, pick corporate representatives the jurors can relate to. Show that, if you deal unjustly with the company, you unjustly penalize the good person sitting before you in the witness box or at the defendant's table. Remember that the ear defers to the eye, so pick folks who look sympathetic as well. The more avuncular, the better.

- For media appearances, likewise pick spokespersons who sound human when they talk, and who don't sound as if they've memorized formal corporate statements. For TV appearances, sympathetic-looking spokespersons are, again, worth their weight in gold.

- For both court and media appearances, humanize the company by humanizing its legal counsel. "I'm a mother of four, stepmother of two, and grandmother of five, and I don't mind using that fact to help my client," says Kimball. "I was born in Brooklyn and I grew up on the South Side of Chicago. I know more than most people what the terror of violence is all about."

For complex product cases, Kimball has also found a way to

make sure she's communicating with the world in a way the world can understand: She rehearses arguments for her family and friends. If they can understand her, chances are that jurors and reporters will too.

With reporters, she speaks slowly and often repeats herself to make sure her points get across. "I don't worry if I don't stay on the reporter's point," she says. "It's not the reporter's question that will help the case. It's my answer."

So Don't Forget...

Here are five simple rules to guide media strategy during a product liability crisis...

- Focus your theme. The same story you tell to the jury, you can tell to the press. Base the theme on solid research and incontrovertible fact, but keep it simple, simple, simple.

- Watch your back. Product cases are often politically motivated or assume political significance. Take the bull by the horns with themes and message points that encourage impartiality even among partisan observers.

- Put on a human face. Jurors love corporate spokespersons who remind them of Walter Cronkite. Ditto TV audiences.

- Vary the messages. Different industries require different messages, as do different kinds of cases.

- The same simple assertion that benefits your company in a single case can be disastrous when the company is simultaneously litigating ten thousand similar cases.

ELEVEN

Special Agendas...Gearing Press Relations to Specific Crisis Areas

T hus far we've looked at policies and procedures that affect media relations in the corridors of corporate power. We've also looked at some very peculiar media dynamics that have driven certain highly sensitive and controversial industries.

Every area of legal exposure, however, entails some special media considerations of its own, irrespective of the industry in which your company is involved.

Think in terms of how your lawyers market themselves to you. When they present themselves as "industry legal teams," with track records serving gun manufacturers or car companies or tobacco, they need to gear their thinking about the media to those industry situations. But, attorneys also market themselves as antitrust experts or bankruptcy practitioners or securities litigators. Media relations play out uniquely for each specific practice area.

It is beyond our scope to look at the media issues peculiar to every legal practice area. However, by reviewing a few of those areas, we can get a sense of how different substantive skill sets apply in each instance, and the subtle extent to which one area of concern differs from another.

We need look no further than antitrust, bankruptcy, and securities litigation for telling hints as to how and why media management should be tailored to accommodate disparate problems.

ANTITRUST: IT'S ALL ABOUT MEDIA

There is no legal area more directly affected by media coverage or where there is a greater obligation to understand and fine-tune media relations than antitrust. It's a fact that might at first blush seem grossly overstated, if not completely incongruous, particularly since many newspaper readers don't even know what antitrust is.

But think it through.

Antitrust law is soft. Different administrations interpret it differently. During the Nixon Administration, corporate kingpins felt the all-probing sting of antitrust law. During the Reagan Administration, antitrust law barely existed.

Even with product liability, there are limits to the impact of media. According to the law, a company is found liable or not found liable, often by conscientious juries whose personal sympathies may not be reflected in their decisions. By contrast, antitrust regulators are freer to act in direct response to what they perceive—subjectively—as corporate good citizenship, as well as to what they perceive as the "best interests of the consumer."

That means, more than other regulators, the folks at DOJ or FTC or at state agencies will bald-facedly form their opinions and determine their official actions on the basis of what they read in the newspapers or see on television. They're allowed to!

Not just regulators, but the Senators who write letters to the agencies are directly affected by a corporation's reputation as formed by the media. Observers point to companies like Computer Associates whose "aggressive" reputations among reporters make life more complicated every time they target a new acquisition.

The attorneys representing companies under scrutiny frequently become spokespersons for their clients and, as Mark Ostrau suggests, their credibility inside the regulatory agency is directly affected as a result. Lawyers with credibility have more leeway in negotiations. Lawyers without credibility are often limited to playing adversarial roles with the regulators.

Ostrau, an antitrust partner at Fenwick & West in Silicon Valley, points out that prosecutorial discretion is directly affected by public opinion and media track records. "Gun jumping" is a case in point, explains Ostrau. Acquirer companies often want to involve themselves in the management or the decision-making at targeted acquisitions before the government has completely finished approving the deal. Doing so can be a clear Hart-Scott-Rodino violation, but whether or not the government will act in such cases is always unclear.

Public reputation is a decisive factor.

Bad PR in antitrust matters can be disastrous. Everybody is a potential plaintiff, as Ostrau points out. Local AGs read the national press and, if they see a case going badly for a company, the news can inspire state action. The AGs, as political animals, are monitoring local popular sentiment as well, so a large company cannot afford to high-hand newspapers in Des Moines or Tacoma.

Media savvy is thus something that antitrust lawyers owe their clients, not as an addendum to their legal practice, but as a definitive component of that legal practice. Ostrau articulates the essential best practices:

- Understand that there are multiple audiences, all of them important. The consumer feeds the politician who feeds the regulator. Make sure your message points fly at the grass-roots level.

- Focus all message points on consumer interest, which is the heart and soul of antitrust decision-making. Why does your position mean better products and services at lower cost?

(Continued on page 157)

The Mother of All Antitrust Cases

You may recall that press coverage of the government's antitrust case against Microsoft was constant, protracted, and in-depth, or at least more in-depth than for any other antitrust case since Teddy Roosevelt went after J.P. Morgan.

Anything less than an amiable and cooperative public posture in an antitrust case is, as a general rule, totally ill advised. Public truculence only makes the regulators more aggressive and the judges more hostile. Yet general rules can be subject to stark reversal when it comes to media strategy.

During much of the case, observers like Mark Ostrau, an antitrust partner at Fenwick & West, tended to believe that Microsoft's press strategy was as perilously obdurate as the business strategy that landed the behemoth in hot water in the first place. They saw nothing but negatives in the company's frequently bumptious refusals to comment or, when it did deign to comment, in its self-serving renditions of breaking case developments.

In retrospect, Ostrau isn't so sure. "Microsoft stayed on message all the time," he says. Their position, like it or not, had the virtue of consistency. True, they almost forced Congress to act by digging in so deeply. Yet, adds Ostrau, as risky as the strategy was, it showed a critical awareness of multiple potential plaintiffs. They were not going to give an inch, apparently because the company and its lawyers understood that, were they to do so, causes of action could spring up like weeds throughout the country.

Sullivan & Cromwell, the New York legal giant representing Microsoft, also has a history of stonewalling the press, and the firm never has paid much of a price for doing so. Their inveterate media "strategy" wasn't broken, so neither the client nor its lawyers were going to try and fix it.

According to Ostrau, an alternative strategy would have been to say to the world, "'Here's an acceptable solution to the problem. We were too aggressive. We will not engage in further exclusive dealing.'" That too might have worked, says Ostrau, had the company mounted a PR campaign to "steer opinion" in favor of the partial solution.

And—the essence of all antitrust PR—such an alternative campaign would have had to hit hard on consumer interest, underscoring the fact that a breakup would produce inferior technology at higher cost. Even amid such monumental litigation, antitrust PR is really just a glorified commercial.

"Here's our idea. Here's why it's the best deal for consumers." Period!

(Continued from page 155)

- Tell stories! The best way to prove that your position is in the best interest of the consumer is with narrative examples that show what will happen as a result of, say, a proposed merger. Then, let the reader connect the dots. "When this car company buys that paint company, it will save millions by using its own product for body work. That means savings for customers and returns for shareholders."

One effective approach, applicable to many business cases but particularly to antitrust litigation, is to show that it is the government—not the company—that is roiling the waters, attempting to challenge, if not altogether transform, normal and acceptable business behavior. "Where the government is trying to establish a novel legal proposition, one can certainly say the case is built on an untried theory," says James Eiszner, who heads up the antitrust practice at Shook, Hardy & Bacon in Kansas City, Missouri. "If, as in the Microsoft case, there is good evidence that the government's case will 'stifle innovation,' then that is a smart thing to say as well."

Such an argument puts the burden of proof on the government to show why, in an area like antitrust where customer satisfaction is the ultimate tribunal, upsetting corporate apple carts would be in anybody's interest (other than the regulators who must tinker with markets in order to justify their jobs).

There is a most peculiar variable affecting the antitrust media market. As we've seen, as antitrust law is subject to vagueness and subjectivity, lawyers who comment on cases are often doing so not on the basis of what a particular law says, but of what they think is the critical consumer-oriented issue.

If regulators can be swayed by public opinion, lawyers commenting in the press are swayed by client interests. Gary Reback, formerly a partner at Wilson, Sonsini, Goodrich & Rosati, has been aggressively attacking Microsoft for years. In fact, he represents Microsoft's chief competitors and doesn't mind admitting it.

Likewise, a reporter once asked Ostrau, while he was commenting on the Microsoft case, if he represented any Microsoft competitors. "I'm a lawyer in Silicon Valley," Ostrau responded. "Who do you think I represent?

"I think the good reporters treat us like the regulators treat us when we're giving them our opinions," says Ostrau. "They look for the kernels of truth, and treat the rest of it with a grain of salt."

BANKRUPTCY: BAD NEWS EARLY AND OFTEN

Regardless of whether they're creditors or debtors, companies in bankruptcy face unique media problems. First, they have to define some angle of interest to the press regarding cases that are often purely procedural. Second, to make the story media-genic, they have to identify good guys and bad guys when often the only guys involved are broke guys.

"Creditors don't approach full victory," says Bill Rochelle, an editor-at-large for Bloomberg News who writes a daily column on bankruptcy. "So it's difficult to come up with a story."

One lawyer who came up with many such stories was Harvey Miller, a longtime favorite of reporters covering bankruptcy matters. A partner at Weil, Gotshal & Manges, Miller marketed himself as the nation's pre-eminent bankruptcy lawyer (which was probably true), thereby becoming the go-to source on any bankruptcy issue that could possibly interest the media and the public. Miller cultivated a mystique of sorts, based on a rather distinctive personality style, while exploiting media interest in workouts for high-profile clients such as Macy's.

The salient media problem for bankruptcy attorneys is that bankruptcy is mainly bad news. The press loves bad news—the proverbial "Plane Lands Safely" won't sell newspapers—and attorneys and their creditor clients enmeshed in the negative coverage don't usually benefit as a result. They may even be the messengers blamed for the message or tarred by it.

On the debtors' side, "the PR is God-awful," says Rochelle. "One press release after another says the situation is 'terribly difficult' or predicts a 'great signal victory ahead.' No one can ever be quite sure what 'great signal victory' they're talking about."

Interestingly, however, media opportunities have opened up for bankruptcy attorneys in the wake of the 2002 corporate scandals. John Lee, a partner at Andrews & Kurth in Houston, points out that debtor representation can be parlayed into favorable press coverage if the attorney makes a case, not just for the client, but for innocent people affected by the bankruptcy.

"Judges read that kind of coverage," says Lee.

Importantly, such messages directly address the primary challenge facing bankruptcy attorneys, which is to make themselves and their clients sympathetic to a public that's just as likely to panic in the face of financial collapse as acknowledge the quality of the professionals working to minimize the damage.

Rochelle points toward a fundamental media strategy for companies in bankruptcy or teetering on the edge. "Get out the bad news early and keep repeating it. Bad news becomes old news."

It's a counter-intuitive strategy in many ways, but one that directly addresses the peculiar nature of bankruptcy practice.

(Continued on page 161)

Soup to Nuts: Media as a Bankruptcy Case Strategy

The recent corporate scandals ending in bankruptcy have made bankruptcy a palpably more colorful media topic, even as the stakes zoom tangibly higher. For better or worse, companies and their attorneys are therefore finding a more avid, responsive press.

John Lee, a partner at Andrews & Kurth in Houston, offers a telling example of how to exploit that interest. Lee launched a fervid media campaign on behalf of Vlasic Foods International, a bankrupt company spun off by the Campbell Soup Company. Campbell's alleged motive was to unload a problem business and transfer as many of its debts to Vlasic as it could get away with by manipulating the financial results and projections of the subsidiary business.

Lee sent out a press release in August 2002, fortunate timing as it coincided with the Enron scandal. His media strategy would directly support his litigation strategy, exponentially increasing the pressure on Campbell, and on the auditors, so that, even should the case be appealed, a powerful climate of opinion would have been created.

Here was a bankruptcy case with real good guys and bad guys. In the wake of the 2002 corporate scandals, Lee was able to quadruple the impact of the press coverage on all directly interested audiences.

Lee also broke a fundamental media rule, but shrewdly so. Brevity is usually the best practice, and that certainly applies to press releases. Journalists often don't read press releases at all, and your best chance at getting their attention is with a few short newsworthy paragraphs. But Lee signed off on a very long release that marshaled evidence against Campbell as if it were the complaint itself.

"We wrestled with the press release," says Lee. "We knew

we had to be careful, because [Campbell] would have loved to sue us for saying the wrong thing. But, with so much evidence, we decided the best approach was to communicate the enormity of the case, and that the best way to do that was by laying it all out."

Result: In the aftermath of the press release, Vlasic's side was sympathetically reported by *Reuters* and *The Wall Street Journal*. Best of all, National Public Radio did a primetime segment that featured music. A singing group chirped,

Mmm mmm bad, mmm mmm bad
That's what Campbell's soups are
Mmm mmm bad.

PR professionals have a term for that kind of coverage. It's called a "home run."

(Continued from page 159)

SECURITIES LITIGATION: UPPING THE ANTE

For securities litigators, the art of media relations is the same as for any other kind of attorney, only more so. Indeed, if there is a peculiar circumstance distinguishing crisis management in this area, it's the mind-boggling consequences of media coverage. In this area of the law, underscore every one of our media lessons, and every one of our best media practices, many times over.

Michael J. Missal, a partner in the Washington, D.C. office of Kirkpatrick & Lockhart Preston Gates Ellis LLP, offers a scenario he's seen repeated in case after case. The regulators take a very aggressive approach to an enforcement action and investors, reacting in part to the press coverage, panic. They sell. The matter is resolved and the market goes up. The investors have locked in their losses.

In one case, Missal says the sell-off was $2 billion. There's also a class action suit lurking behind every unfavorable published word, not just in *The Wall Street Journal,* but on some obscure online information service as well. In securities litigation, there's a plaintiffs' bar second to none in rapacity and for expert *sub rosa* media manipulation.

In such an environment, there's no substitute for proactive media outreach. Securities litigators and, as appropriate, the companies they represent must broaden and deepen their relationships with the reporters in the field. Equally crucial is to anticipate a worst-case scenario in every situation and, as Missal strongly advises, take steps to educate the relevant reporters as to the actual facts of your case.

Another characteristic distinguishing this area is that the cases are not only enormously high-stakes, but enormously complex as well. Left to their own devices, even seasoned business reporters are liable to get it all wrong. The solution is to assume that, in the best interests of your client, reporters need to be educated—and without making them feel they're the village idiots.

In a down market, proactive solutions are especially imperative as the whole world is looking for scapegoats. Work the press aggressively, Missal advises. For example:

- Follow up on all allegations. Advise reporters when the allegations are less harsh than they might seem in statements issued by the regulators. Your goal is to always convince the press that there's no real story here, or much less of one than might appear at first glance.

- When reporters get it wrong, don't recriminate, but do point out their errors. It will mean a better chance next time—and there will always be a next time—to educate the writers or vet what they're going to publish before they publish it.

- Always be available as a free source of information to reporters, with no concern over whether or not they're going to cite you as an expert in their articles. You maintain enormous credibility by unselfishly helping out on matters where you're disinterested.

(Continued on page 164)

From Mole Hill to Media Mountain

When Turner Communications hired Michael Milken as a consultant in the mid-1990s, you'd have thought from the coverage in newspapers throughout the United States that it was the biggest story since he and Boesky were convicted in the first place.

Milken, of course, was barred from trading in securities. He was still on probation when Ted Turner enlisted him. The intense press coverage, which clearly pointed toward a blatant violation of the ban, kicked off an investigation by both the DOJ and SEC.

In fact, Milken was not trading in securities. He was merely acting as a consultant. As a source close to the situation now reflects, Turner's response was a classic case of helpless reaction to the media when a methodically proactive approach was needed.

Effective early media outreach would have ideally relied on a simple analogy to deflect the story. Analogize Milken to anyone who acts as a liaison and collects a finder's fee for his efforts. The intricacies of securities law would have been boiled down to just such basics, leaving little room to charge Milken with dealing or Turner with complicity.

The reinforcing point would then have been to tell reporters what Milken would have actually needed to do to break the law. Thus do you box in the reporters by anticipating their skepticism. By describing what a violation would look like, you reassure them that they're not missing something in the situation that's incriminatory. You've covered all ends of the imbroglio without recourse to a single legal Arcanum.

Yes, the regulators would have read the results in the press and acted accordingly. And, a story on page 5 instead of page 1, even were it to still question the propriety of the engagement, would have been far less likely to catalyze official action.

(Continued from page 162)

A proactive media approach is all the more critical to balance the constant feed of information from the other side once lawsuits start getting filed. In particular, Milberg Weiss, until its split-up the nation's largest securities plaintiffs' firm, was a veritable media machine.

As Missal points out, some plaintiffs' firms often put the media in touch with seemingly "pathetic" victims of the alleged securities scam. Those pathetic victims may finally turn out to be diversified investors worth seven figures. It's always helpful to steer reporters to the truth if doing so discredits your opponents or opens reporters' eyes as to who is really manipulating them.

So Don't Forget...

Since the dynamics differ from one type of crisis to another, different legal crises areas involve unique challenges when dealing with the media. For example,

- Antitrust practice is media-driven. Antitrust law itself is all about subjective judgment. Anything that gets printed can affect how regulators, politicians, and their constituents regard the company—and can decisively tip the scales on prosecutorial judgment calls.

- Bankruptcy is bad news. The press loves bad news. Your task is to find the social benefit and underscore it in human terms; the retiree whose nest egg is being salvaged, for example. And get the bad news out and keep it out. That way, when there is good news, it's the angle that reporters may likely turn to and focus on.

- Securities litigation translates into billions of dollars. But the law is complex and most reporters get it wrong. Be proactive, be patient, and always look to minimize the import of every enforcement action.

TWELVE

Another Crucial Complication...
How Cultural Differences Affect
Media Management Across Borders

In March 2003, Bayer faced its first trial in defense of the anti-cholesterol drug Baycol. Throughout the trial, plaintiff's lawyer Mikal Watts took every opportunity to remind the jury that Bayer is a foreign (German) company.

Under the circumstances, Watts had good reason to wield a xenophobic cudgel. The trial was occurring in Corpus Christi, Texas, a reputedly "plaintiff-friendly" haven and a region known for strong protectionist sensibilities. Yet, the tactic failed. It failed, in part, because Bayer Aspirin has been, for decades, too much a constant of American consumer life to arouse any dread of economic infiltration. But the tactic also failed because the jurors were perhaps too intelligent to rise to the bait. There had been no anti-German screeds in the Texas press, nor might the jury have been affected if there were.

There are innumerable gradations on the cross-border spectrum. Lawyers, for example, will find that a partner defection from one law firm to another, or some other typical industry event, could inspire glaring tabloid-like headlines and speculation in the UK legal press. In the United States, *American Lawyer* or *The National Law Journal* might yawn off the same event.

In any event, no discussion of media relations in a global legal marketplace is complete without a look at how companies can make crucial adjustments to indigenous media cultures and, in so doing, achieve better results for clients facing crises or lawsuits abroad.

Let's consider what happens to potentially unpopular foreign clients under scrutiny in the United States.

FINDING COMMON AGENDAS

U.S. media outlets are usually too sophisticated to want or need to attack non-American litigants in the United States. Even if a foreign company has been blithely ignoring SEC regulations, the readers of *The Wall Street Journal* won't necessarily be any more outraged by the reported malfeasance than by the activities of Mr. Skilling or Ms. Stewart. Those readers do business with foreigners every day.

Yet even purportedly fair newspapers like *The New York Times* or *The Washington Post* may sometimes find that your client's nationality is an issue and sometimes legitimately so. The lawsuit or crisis at hand may be relevant to current trade policy, for example. Or, the situation has resulted in such strong public opprobrium related to national or political factors that the public reaction itself is newsworthy.

Then there are the countless other media outlets that directly reflect, and often cater to, their readers' national or regional fears. When BP Petroleum pulled out of Cleveland, Ohio a few years back and thousands of jobs were lost, the local media was much more hostile than if it had been Exxon Mobil. When President Chirac does not go to war in Iraq, a French company may have a tough time winning a lawsuit in Cody, Wyoming.

And, if subtly anti-foreign pressure is being exerted against your client by the President of the United States, then, as Thomas Wilner discovered, you've got a real media problem. Wilner, a partner in the Washington, D.C. office of Shearman & Sterling, found a surprisingly inquiring press in the mid-1990s when he was representing Mexican vegetable growers in a trade dispute with Florida.

At issue were Mexican exports competing with Florida tomatoes. Normally, The Tomato War might have been relegated to the back of the business section, except in *The Miami Herald* and other Florida publications. But the timing was not propitious. President Clinton was up for reelection and dead set on carrying Florida. The Presidential team went to the press.

In such situations, Wilner will usually take two immediate steps. "The first thing I do is list all my messages," he says. These are the substantive points that stand the best chance of getting heard on the company's behalf. "The next thing I do is list all the possible messengers," including client representatives, experts, supportive third parties, and himself. Often, Wilner advises, the attorneys in his cases are the spokespersons actually preferred by reporters.

Since such situations entail a battle over public opinion, and involve public perceptions of foreign interests, the messages are seldom strictly about points of law. They are social and political.

As social and political messages, they must in some way overcome or defuse the implicit chauvinism of the opposition, or the opposition's powerful (and often legitimate) focus on local jobs and local interests. When we look at Wilner's campaigns over the years on behalf of foreign companies in the United States, we find a shrewd pattern of changing the agenda. In other words, he pursues a different but equally relevant political discussion in which reporters and the public are likelier to be on his side.

The tomato fracas is a case in point. Wilner went to the press with alternatives to the "Mexican Tomato Growers Are Snatching Revenue from American Tomato Growers" message. In particular:

- Florida's tomatoes are "gas green," meaning treated with chemical substances. Mexican tomatoes are red right off the vine. They're better for the environment. They're better for your health.

(Continued on page 169)

A Cartel In Perspective

It's challenging enough to prevail in the media on behalf of a foreign client when powerful political interests line up against you. It's profoundly more difficult when the foreign interests have been vilified from the outset.

Thomas Wilner, a partner in the Washington, D.C. office of Shearman & Sterling, has represented the Organization of Petroleum Exporting Countries (OPEC) in antitrust cases in the District of Columbia and a federal court in Alabama. From a media standpoint, he faced two problems. One is the residual hostility some media sources and the public harbor against OPEC, dating back to the oil crisis of the 1970s. The other is that the suits were filed by David Boies, a master of media relations.

Wilner prevailed in both lawsuits—as of this writing, they're on appeal—in part because he developed pointed messages that anticipated and defused anti-OPEC sentiment. Wilner advised a low media profile and did not seek to litigate the cases in public. But he readied himself for media inquiries, not with legal arguments, but with politically sensitive points designed to put OPEC itself in proper context.

- OPEC nations are poor. For most, oil is their one natural resource. For Nigeria, it's 80 percent of the economy.

- It's economic imperialism to apply our laws to how other countries handle their own resources in the global market.

- The United States behaves no differently with its own resources in some cases. For example, the embargo on Cuba guarantees the United States an OPEC-like stranglehold on sugar.

- Americans buy gas-guzzling vehicles. When we do that, we exacerbate the problem.

Such messages had a decisive effect. Coverage by the *Associated Press* and *The New York Times* has been supportive.

(*Continued from page 167*)

- These red right-off-the-vine tomatoes are available to Americans only from Mexico. Most Americans, including Floridians, prefer the Mexican tomatoes. The opposition is interfering with free market choice.

- The tomato growers in Mexico are very, very poor. The tomato growers in Florida are very, very rich. They have also been charged with polluting the Everglades.

Any one of these message points might not have sufficed to overcome Florida's impulse to protect Floridian interests. No single argument might have defused instinctive media antipathy to foreign interests. But taken together, they formed a broadly sympathetic political platform that won the media war. When a Clinton lieutenant talked with *The Chicago Tribune*, the paper put him on the defensive and wouldn't let him move past the issue.

The case settled on terms mutually favorable to Mexico and Florida, and Clinton carried Florida anyway. "It was one of my greatest accomplishments," teases Wilner.

Here, it was the message points themselves that decisively changed a specific political landscape in favor of a foreign party. In a more recent fight with another U.S. President, it was the use of the right spokespersons that leveled the playing field.

When George W. Bush introduced steel tariffs, Wilner's overriding goal on behalf of Arcelor, a Belgian/French/Spanish steel company, was to show that tariffs are bad for the U.S. economy. An immediate goal was at least to win key exclusions for as many of the client's products as possible.

Wilner commissioned an economic study that supported the general anti-tariff message, which was well received by the press, since the economist who worked on it was an articulate messenger. Support from the National Retail Federation was likewise salutary.

But the real victory for the client may have occurred more at the local level, because the spokespersons were local residents who told how badly they'd be hurt by having to pay more for specific products that Arcelor was providing.

The message reversed the protectionist impact: To protect Americans, we must liberalize foreign imports. But the message was also significantly enhanced because the case that was made to the media was not argued theoretically by lawyers or economists, but by average American citizens.

The politicians may have listened to a message about the macro effects of tariffs on the economy delivered by an expert spokesperson. But they really heard the message about local consequences delivered by local people in local media. Result: More Arcelor products were excluded from the tariffs than those of any other affected foreign steel concern.

TARGET EUROPE

If the Battle of Waterloo was won on the proverbial playing fields of Eton, a fight just across the Channel waged by Arco Chemical before the European Commission over a site license was won in the editorial columns of the *Financial Times*.

For companies doing business on foreign soil, one critical media objective is to secure broad political support. It is indeed a political struggle, all about changing the agenda and replacing one ideological hot button with another. We've looked at how such cases play out in the United States. They may well play out the same way in any nation. Only the specific hot buttons vary from country to country.

A very different issue in cross-border media management is the use of media to directly affect decision-makers. Here, the media strategy must sometimes be very finely tuned because we're not just taking aim at an amorphous creature called public opinion. We can't just plaster the Sunday Supplements and hope for the best. We must learn instead about each media market, about what the decision-makers actually read, and about how substantive discussions must be packaged for maximum impact.

Media target marketing is especially well-advised in Europe. According to Ian Forrester, a partner in the Brussels office of White & Case, European decision-makers are circumspect about what they read and which publications they allow to affect their decisions.

For antitrust cases in Europe, "decision-makers" most often means the European Commission, while the European courts are not so susceptible to direct media influence as courts in the United States. There are no jury pools to influence, and thus no reason for corporations to curry public favor in order to win, say, a product liability case. Non-European companies should certainly worry about how the European press characterizes them—their reputations, their products, their services—for all the obvious marketing reasons. But there isn't usually a direct connection between public opinion and case outcome.

> "*Vox populi* is not an issue for the courts," says Ian Forrester, a partner in the Brussels office of White & Case. "But I am in no doubt that the European Commission is sensitive to how things appear to the public and in the media" on all specific issues related to their policy-making function.

"*Vox populi* is not an issue for the courts," says Forrester. "But I am in no doubt that the European Commission is sensitive to how things appear to the public and in the media" on all specific issues related to their policy-making function.

The question is: Which public? Which media?

As we have seen, for antitrust cases in the United States, companies can reach decision-makers through any number of media venues, even including local dailies in smaller cities. In the United States, a shotgun approach over time can be a very effective ongoing weapon for or against, say, Microsoft. In Europe, a company that has a lot riding on EC policy decisions ought to be hiring lawyers and media advisors who know precisely which media to play and when. Otherwise the message never gets through.

That Arco case, handled by Forrester, is illustrative. Arco, facing the prohibition of single-plant limits on site licensing of technology, took its argument to the EC. But as Forrester interpreted the Commission's leanings during the early stages of the case, his client's position was likely to be rejected. It was at that point, with less to lose, that he helped arrange for the *Financial Times* to run a debate on the subject.

The debate was neither tendentious nor one-sided. All points of view were covered in what Forrester describes as a lively and informed discussion. Yet Forrester says he is now "quite confident" the *Financial Times* feature turned the tide in favor of Arco as the comments there by informed supporters of the company's position provided crucial additional public endorsement.

The point, though, is that it was the *Financial Times*, not *The Times of London*. "They [the EC] don't read *The New York Times* [either]. They might see *The Wall Street Journal Online*," says Forrester, but they don't read the newspaper with any regularity.

According to Forrester, the Commissioners do read *Le Monde, Frankfurter Allegemeine Zeitung,* and *Neue Zürcher Zeitung,* a major Swiss newspaper with an international readership, as well as the *Financial Times.*

Depending on the kind of case, Forrester might also call specialty writers at the *European Voice,* a Brussels- and London-based weekly launched by the publishers of *The Economist* in 1995 to cover EC regulatory and political developments. He might also call various writers at Agence Europe in Brussels, which puts out a number of publications monitoring the EC, including an important update called *Europe Daily Bulletin.*

In Europe, clients expect their attorneys to call the press in order to affect EC decisions, especially when things seem to be going badly, as in Forrester's Arco matter. The art of the press interview itself does not vary as radically from country to country as one might expect. The nuances of personal communications change according to culture, of course, but there are abiding professional similarities among journalists. Some of the same best practices apply everywhere.

For example, Forrester is careful with all reporters to emphasize during an interview when he is on the record and when he is not. "I will craft my on-the-record quotes while I am talking to the reporter, and I will ask to check the quotes before the article is published." Reporters worldwide normally honor this request.

Especially for complex business matters, there is a universal need to simplify. Journalists in France are as bemused by legalese as journalists in New York, and the same sound bites that get the job done for you and your client in one country will do so in another as well—no matter how sophisticated the outlet.

So Don't Forget...

Cross-border media relations is about protecting your company in potentially hostile environments. It's all about politics.

- Change the message. Foreigner-as-enemy is just one message. Craft alternative messages that shift the debate and appeal to popular public agendas that serve the client's interests.

- Enlist third-party support. The right spokespersons will identify your company as being in the same camp as local interests. It's no longer us-against-them when some of "us" have the same goals.

- Pick your targets. In Europe, the regulators are highly susceptible to media influence but there are just a handful of publications where you can exert that influence.

- Follow the same rules. Brevity is everywhere the soul of wit and all readers respond best to sound bites. Journalists in most countries that have a free press play the same game. They've all got deadlines, and they all know the difference between on and off the record.

THIRTEEN

Law Firms in Trouble: Unique Media Strategies for a Unique Market

L et's take a look at a few less than pleasant realities confronting law firms in the 21st century.

First, there have always been crooked attorneys and incompetent attorneys, and they were just as fair game for reporters in 1903 as in 2003. However, with the growth of civil litigation in our lifetime, law firms themselves have also become targets simply because, for plaintiffs' attorneys, that's where the money is. If an attorney has merely said hello to Skilling or Fastow during the last few years, his or her entire firm may now be named in some class action somewhere.

Second, it's not just plaintiffs' firms fishing in deep pockets. In the 1990s, one law firm after another fell victim to the FDIC and its Office of Thrift Supervision as the government sued just about everyone who ever represented S&L kingpin Charles Keating or other failed thrift operators throughout the country. Many thousands of average citizens had lost their money and the political pressure to punish all involved parties was intense.

New York's Kaye, Scholer, Fierman, Hays & Handler was the worst-hit law firm. The firm argued that its representation of Keating was zealous advocacy, not only permitted, but mandated, under the professional canons. It would have cost a fortune to prove it, however, so the firm finally settled, although not before it was featured several times on the front page of *The New York Times* as well as in other major newspapers.

Government interest in allegedly errant law firms continues. Right now Enron-involved law firms are DOJ and SEC targets, not just plaintiffs' targets in civil litigation. In the current environment, lawyer-client confidentiality is under siege and any erosion of that sacred principle means only more personal liability for lawyers and their firms.

Third, the *American Lawyer* publishes law firms' per-partner profits every year. That editorial feature has changed the complexion of the American legal profession more profoundly than any other single development in its history. It means that everyone can peek into your business and draw whatever conclusions they want as to your competitive viability. Worse, it has made for exponentially greater numbers of partner defections as attorneys shift from reportedly less profitable firms to others reportedly more profitable.

Ideally, a partner departure will only rate a sentence or two in a local legal newspaper. The good news is that, because there are so many partner defections, it takes a little more than the event itself to make it newsworthy. The bad news is that the events often are newsworthy because the partner is so high-profile, because the departure signals stormy weather for the firm, or because a whole practice group has left.

Moreover, partner defections are sometimes so acrimonious that they can generate any number of ancillary problems as well. In the late 1980s, firms tried hard to punish defecting partners by denying portions of their receivables based on non-compete clauses in partnership agreements. A banner case was the suit filed by New York's now-defunct Lord, Day & Lord against a tax partner who left the firm and took a major client, *The New York Times*, with him. Lord, Day did not prevail.

(Continued on page 178)

A Universal Problem

One thing law firms in trouble have going for them is a legal press that may at times be unfair but is at least fairly sophisticated, especially when it comes to marketplace trends.

Legal reporters know the problems attendant with growth. They know that, as law firms expand, it becomes increasingly difficult to maintain a seamless professional culture or to adequately monitor the behavior of all their partners.

Legal reporters will still blame firms for breakdowns, and they should. But their understanding of the market can at least temper their philippics when law firms articulate a comprehensive but succinct message to address the crisis and deliver it sympathetically.

A case in point is a global law firm that was dismayed to learn that one of its partners was stealing immense amounts of money. The attorney's practice was so abstruse that it would have been hard to detect the malfeasance under any circumstances. With the firm's attorney ranks then in excess of 700, the criminal was able to escape unnoticed for quite a while.

Good move number one: The law firm made no attempt to deny the problem or to avoid press calls.

Good move number two: The managing partner is a soft-spoken, somewhat avuncular person, with the wise but unprepossessing tone of a Walter Cronkite.

Good move number three: The firm really only had one message point, but it was powerful. *If it can happen here, it can happen anywhere.*

For seasoned legal reporters, that message was both credible and comprehensive. On the one hand, it made the story larger than the firm itself. It made their crisis a profession-wide crisis, which means the discussion of it in the press was not a down-and-dirty ferreting out of firm-specific facts. Instead, it was a discussion of a universal problem, of which this particular firm was just one example.

Finally, the message point reinforced the fundamental excellence of the firm itself by reminding reporters and their readers that the real significance of the scandal was that it actually happened to such a wonderful organization.

One publication even ran the message point as the headline of the story.

(*Continued from page 176*)

It was an ill-advised effort in any event, as it ultimately drew negative press attention to Lord, Day. It's just unseemly for attorneys to sue each other. The legal press loves it, but clients don't. "Law firms really ought to settle these things as fast as they can," says Leslie Corwin, a partner in the New York office of Greenberg Traurig, who points out that restrictive covenants are just not enforceable in the legal industry.

Corwin should know. He has represented both partners and firms on both sides of diverse partnership disputes. Most famously, in the 1980s, he represented Evan Dawson, a partner dismissed by White & Case.

Finally, there is an overriding consideration that makes media relations during any law firm crisis uniquely less tractable than with other organizations. The judgment against Lord, Day was based, to a substantial degree, on the fundamental principle that, by enforcing non-compete clauses, law firms deny clients their basic right to free choice of counsel.

In a sense, that emphasis on client rights reverberates in any discussion of the options law firms have for handling public imbroglios, including what they can and cannot say to the press. Law is a thoroughly client-driven business, after all, and clients maintain not just the right to choose counsel, but to confidentiality as well.

Law firms' lives are therefore not their own. Any press strategy must be tempered by what's best for a client even when it may not be the best strategy for the firm itself.

OPTIMAL MIDDLE GROUND

At the same time, a virtual paranoia about how clients will react to public comments by their attorneys paralyzes many firms confronted with crisis. The result is that they finally exert no control over what reporters wind up writing and what the marketplace winds up thinking.

Conversely, attorneys are also inclined to want to control messages. It's an inclination that often makes them less than ideal press sources in general. Such extreme circumspection can prove utterly crippling if the news topic at hand is a departed partner or an SEC investigation or a client representation that went seriously awry.

As media attention will predictably continue to increase, both in the legal and general press, it is therefore imperative that law firms evolve media plans and best media practices, just as their clients in the tobacco or gun industries have done under the withering scrutiny of regulators and reporters. For law firms, such planning must walk a delicate middle ground and take careful measure of client interest even as it maximizes the law firm's message about itself.

Here are Les Corwin's prescriptions for law firms, to be administered as prophylaxis before a crisis occurs and to control the damage once the bad news goes public.

Codify your policy

All organizations need to designate crisis spokespersons and, as appropriate, exclusively limit press access to that spokesperson. With law firms, the need is acute. In a flat and politically charged organization, random and contradictory statements by partners can be deadly. The flip side of law firm paralysis is law firm entropy; that is, any number of self-justifying or self-interested partners may feel no constraint about taking their personal agenda to the press or responding on their own to random press inquiries.

Corwin offers a definitive solution that takes into account these unique political vagaries that can roil a law firm in crisis: Put it in your partnership agreement! "The partnership agreement itself should contain a crisis clause that assigns exclusive authority to a single person, usually the managing partner, to speak for the firm," says Corwin.

The clause could also include a mechanism defining a crisis. For example, it can stipulate that any litigation involving the firm itself constitutes a crisis. Depending on the firm, it can also stipulate that any presumably negative event affecting the firm, even the defection of a single partner, triggers the crisis clause.

The idea is additionally salutary in light of attorneys' typical reverence for the written word and its binding contractual impact. In lieu of a crisis clause in the partnership agreement, managing partners typically send out memoranda to the partnership as crises occur, warning against speaking to the press and commanding every single member of the firm to direct all press inquiries to his or her office.

Such memoranda are always a good idea, but if they're not backed up by a solemn declaration in the partnership agreement, they are perceived more as tactical stopgaps than ironclad policy.

The buck stops here

As the firm spokesperson, the managing partner should be trained to deal with the press. (Formal media training is available from outside sources.) Inexplicably, law firms often choose their leaders with absolutely no regard for their ability to communicate with the outside world, either during crises or in the normal course of business. It should be as basic a job skill as the ability to read a financial statement.

The crisis clause may include an option for the managing partner to also designate additional spokespersons should the situation warrant. Corwin advises that the law firm's outside counsel is often a wise choice, particularly if the managing partner is personally at risk in a crisis or too close to a situation to maintain sufficient equilibrium.

Reporters know a rudderless ship when they see one. When

the *American Lawyer* did a feature over a decade ago on Boston's ill-fated Gaston & Snow, reporter Peter Carbonari turned up at the firm and, as Corwin recalls, "said, 'take me to your leader.' He was shuffled off to [the executive director] some guy who used to work at NYNEX." (Corwin represented one of the partners during the firm's dissolution.)

It seemed as if the managing partner had totally abdicated his role as spokesperson, confirming Carbonari's impression that the firm was floundering. The impression was correct. The managing partner had, in fact, abdicated his leadership role altogether. Attorneys must run law firms and speak for them as well.

Don't let them see it first in the newspaper

There are two specific audiences that you need to immediately speak to at the first whiff of public crisis. The first is internal. The largest corporations in the world take pains to advise their employees when a major scandal or investigation is occurring. For law firms, the need is acute. Your partners feel entitled to that information even more importunately than might high-level executives in a hierarchal corporate organization. If they feel blindsided, the negative effects on the firm, in terms of internal comity, will likely be worse and go on longer than the crisis itself.

At the same time as you are communicating internally, consider contacting every key client you believe might care one way or another about the unfolding crisis. At the very least, it's a courtesy and relationship-building gesture. At best, it defuses any real concerns clients may have about your ability to continue doing their work.

Enlist third-party support

Once you've contacted clients on the eve of crisis, it then becomes easier to solicit their public statements of support. During its S&L ordeal, Kaye, Scholer's very ability to function as a law firm was directly questioned in the press. The crisis was snowballing, just as it did when Arthur Andersen's clients began doubting the firm's capacity to continue to do business.

Kaye, Scholer's response was to choose a new chairman who made it his business to settle the case as fast as possible. But the firm also directed reporters to important clients, including big ones like Texaco, and friendly general counsel willing to publicly express their confidence in and commitment to the firm.

Such endorsements begin the process of converting negative messages into positive ones. The comments in the press by these in-house supporters were, if nothing more, reminders to the world that Kaye, Scholer did indeed have a blue-chip clientele.

The media tide never did turn dramatically in Kaye, Scholer's favor, but the firm was at least able to convalesce. As the settlement dust cleared, the convalescence included shrewdly placed mentions in the press of attractive new partners in growth areas such as intellectual property joining the firm. The managing partner remained accessible to the press throughout the period.

Many law firms would not have survived. A decade later, Kaye, Scholer remains a strong Manhattan law firm.

Take the initiative

You can be sure that a bad story about your firm will not be ignored; it will be publicly dissected. At law firms, with so many inmates running the asylum, there's seldom enough nerve to tell the story first. But it can sometimes be the best practice for major events like a government investigation (subject to advice from outside counsel) as well as less cataclysmic partner defections or branch office closings.

The advantages are threefold.

First, it takes you off the defensive. Reporters see the story differently when they see you're unafraid to discuss it.

Second, it gives you the first shot at making your point that the investigation is without merit, or that the firm is still strong despite so-and-so's departure for a competitor.

Third, it sets you apart from other law firms. Reporters are often

(*Continued on page 187*)

Issue Management: A Defining Challenge

Some issues have beginnings, middles, and ends. The company expects a controversial event to occur. It fully discloses vital related facts in advance, seeding public opinion before its adversaries can react. The event occurs. There is minimal hue and cry, virtually no litigation, and the company moves on to another issue.

By contrast, there are issues that, because they speak to an organization's core values, have no neat endings and must be managed on a daily basis as well. For corporations and professional service firms, diversity is often the most important case in point.

All other motives aside, organizations presumably pursue racial and gender diversity because it is the right thing to do. That said, the best intentions are often only that...intentions. "The hardest thing about achieving diversity in a corporate context is that most of the people who run corporations are white, male, and straight," says diversity consultant Verna Myers, principal of the Verna Myers Consulting Group, LLC. "No matter how well-intentioned they are, they simply cannot see how successfully implementing a diversity program can actually help them or enhance their businesses."

According to Myers, our corporate fathers really have no way to know because they've never actually lived with or worked with minorities, at least not as peers. "Diversity is social work to them," says Myers. "They may support the larger social objectives, but the personal connection is missing." It's therefore impossible for them to understand it in business terms as a goal that, if fulfilled, will have a tangible and salutary effect on day-to-day operations.

"Without that insight, it becomes commensurately more difficult to make a diversity initiative work, no matter how many best practices are memorized and attempted," adds Myers. "You have to have experienced the value of diversity first-hand."

If business leaders do see direct practical value in diversity, it's because their own customers or clients demand it. Manufacturers, for example, want employee ranks as varied as the consumers they sell to, in part because those consumers demand it. In turn, these businesses expect professional service providers to aggressively pursue diversity and weigh their efforts as a significant factor in retention decisions. For example, the *Houston Chronicle* recently reported (May 13, 2007) that the 27 firms surviving a Shell Oil Co. beauty contest must now "account to Shell for how many female and minority lawyers work on Shell business, for how many hours they work and what they do."

Be advised that the marketplace sees past the "window dressing" and will spot high attrition rates among women and minorities—and, to be sure, so will employees. Indeed, the real issue from a communications standpoint is that the most professional and effective PR campaign—media features on minority executives or websites that highlight racial and gender diversity—can backfire if they paint a persuasive picture for outsiders while the insiders know better.

"Some companies have decided to use actors in their PR because the actual employees they once featured online or in commercials have left or very likely will leave," says Myers. "In other instances, they use real employees, but the tokenism is rampant and obvious."

Results: The slicker the PR, the more distrust it sows among the very people that employers want to retain.

Job candidates, meanwhile, are shrewdly attuned to the word on the street: Is that brokerage house or law firm serious in its commitment? Do minorities and women succeed there? Have they risen to key management posts? Are they given plum assignments? The word on the street is then memorialized online. Any organization that is serious about diversity had better be monitoring the blogosphere where (to mix metaphors) perceptions circulate like wildfire and opinions harden like cement.

Diversity is thus as much a communications challenge as an

HR challenge. Success on both fronts requires daily attention to clearly define and aggressively implement goals. The program must go beyond image. It requires:

✔ Intensive institutional self-analysis, which may include the help of 'outside' diversity consultants. Significantly, such self-analysis is similar to what organizations must also do during crisis situations. They must put all cards on the table and soberly confront every liability. Is a business unit dominated by a good-old-boys mentality? Have racist comments been overheard? Any past EEOC actions or Title VII lawsuits must obviously be revisited and the lessons learned reexamined.

✔ An aggressive diversity plan with specific steps enumerated to assure the accountability of appropriate managers and a mechanism designed to measure results. Measurement is both an internal and external necessity. It shows what still needs to be accomplished and it provides credible data on what has already been accomplished—which can then be included in RFPs, posted online, and communicated to reporters, including trade press reporters covering specific industries and professions.

✔ Promulgate a 'diversity' brand in the marketplace with an internal and external communications plan that draws on all available data, articulates future goals, and, as appropriate, spotlights a range of employees—embracing physically challenged staffers as well as women and minorities, and including both managers and non-managers—who have something special to say about the organization.

Even as some skeptics predictably challenge the quality of the results, others will attack from the other side—questioning the actual value and fairness of diversity itself as an institutional goal. "Diversity backlash" is indeed a recurrent phenomenon.

The backlash may take a cue from *Bakke* and other high-profile cases by asserting the rights of overlooked majority candidates.

Or, as law firms in particular have recently seen, aggressive challenges from some academic quarters tendentiously maintain that minority recruitment lowers standards, that African American lawyers themselves suffer as a result, and that attrition rates actually rise as a direct result of diversity initiatives. In 2004, these conclusions were purportedly supported by research published in the *Stanford Law Review* by UCLA Law School professor Richard Sander. NPR, as well as the cable TV talk shows spotlighted Sander's challenge even as the methodology was being strongly refuted by subsequent quantitative research.

Effective issues management should anticipate such controversy with diversity plans and subsequent branding campaigns that strictly eschew the language of "preference." The diversity program is to be presented in every internal and external venue as a search for excellence—for professionals of every stripe who are demonstrably qualified under existing organizational standards. Diversity recruitment expresses abundance mentality. It is not exclusive. It is not a zero sum game.

Finally, for all their best efforts, some organizations simply cannot show competitive diversity numbers. For these organizations, there is an immediate communications opportunity as well as a challenge. It is the opportunity to communicate heartfelt resolve, provided the organization can underscore specific and credible remedial steps.

At one major law firm, for example, the litigation chair openly acknowledges how disappointed he's been by the numbers of African-American partners recruited and retained. "We hired a Chief Diversity Officer," he told us, "and that Chief Diversity Officer sits in and provides critical input on diversity at every single meeting of our Executive Committee."

In the long run, of course, such best efforts will not be enough and may still seem lackluster. For now, however, the firm is at least showing its intent to sit squarely on the side of the angels. Indeed, professionals of color might find it very much in their interest to identify the firms that *haven't* achieved their goal but that are now so palpably resolved to do so.

In any event, the direct utilization of senior majority executives to truthfully and believably speak to the diversity marketplace is a strategy that diversity consultants like Verna Myers heartily commend—especially as an alternative to glossy features on blacks or women who may not represent the internal corporate reality.

"The problem is getting them to speak in a way that doesn't sound condescending or that doesn't show just how maladroit and uncomfortable they are on this topic," says Myers. "They really need to be well-versed when talking about diversity in public. Otherwise they lose credibility and set back the whole initiative."

(Continued from page 182)

impatient with lawyerly reticence and institutional foot-dragging. A bold, proactive disclosure helps define you as a no-nonsense organization. It suggests that you are well-run and decisive.

Don't fly solo

Corwin believes that the same rule applies in PR as in litigation: Law firms that do not seek outside expertise have their own foolish selves for clients. Outside advisors not only know more about the press than you do, they're dispassionate as well. Their decisions are grounded in reason, suggests Corwin, not self-defensive emotion.

Law firms should pick outside advisors who know the legal market inside and out. There are a finite number of legal publications and you ought to expect your PR people to have personal relationships with reporters at every single one of those publications.

In the UK, reporters bring a tabloid-like ferocity to their coverage of the legal profession. If the London market is at all important to you, expect to be poked at, jeered at, and negatively depicted. You can minimize the damage via London-based PR professionals friendly with editors and reporters at all UK legal publication.

What Do We Say?

The political tinderbox that exists normally at so many law firms makes press relations a uniquely challenging task on all levels. It certainly makes message development difficult. Partners will cavil at this angle; they'll scoff at that angle. Best case scenario, they'll nitpick it to death, changing "glad" to "happy" wherever possible. Ultimately, the managing partner must sign off on all messages in all situations and resolutely stand by them.

When dealing with the general press, assume the reporters know very little about the overall dynamics of how law firms operate in the marketplace, much less the subtle nuances. It is an esoteric business, after all, so prepare to even explain what a practice area is. If you're Kaye, Scholer in the 1990s, don't assume the reporter knows that you were *supposed* to zealously represent Charles Keating. Explain it, carefully and emphatically.

With the legal press, you can assume varying degrees of sophistication, but in most cases, an *American Lawyer* or *National Law Journal* reporter will know quite a bit about the marketplace. You can play such knowledge to your advantage if, for example, you are losing a partner.

Assume the departing partner is not a rainmaker. As Corwin suggests, you can hint to reporters that the departure relates, in part, to the firm's aggressive growth posture. The departing partner—while an extraordinarily talented practitioner—does not fit with the firm's "high standards" in terms of business development, nor does his particular practice "fit in with the firm's goals."

Assume the departing partner is a rainmaker. Here, the firm should remember that the primary readership (aside from directly affected clients) is other attorneys. Corwin suggests an open acknowledgement that the firm will miss the departed lawyer and will be actively looking to replace him or her.

It's a free job advertisement. Most readers won't see weakness, they'll see opportunity if they're at all interested in making a change, particularly for more money, or to go a firm like your own that may have a better profits-per-partner index than their current one.

In other words, the very forces in the legal marketplace that cause law firms such public as well as internal headaches can be played to their benefit, if the firm is organized, coherent, and just a little braver than many law firms usually are.

So Don't Forget...

Law firms have media issues that virtually no other organization faces. Client interests rule and non-compete covenants don't work. To hoe the tough row...

- Include language in your partnership agreement that designates one spokesperson, usually the managing partner, in the event of crisis, and that specifically prohibits press contacts by other partners unless expressly permitted.

- Communicate immediately with all partners, apprising them of the crisis. Communicate immediately with all key clients and, if possible, enlist those clients as supportive press contacts during the crisis.

- Rely on outside media advisors, but be sure that those advisors have good personal relationships with reporters at every important legal publication in the country.

- With general media reporters, assume they know nothing of legal industry dynamics. With legal trade reporters, assume a fair amount of sophistication, and use their knowledge of the profession to support your position.

FOURTEEN

The Immense Significance of Offense in Crisis Communications Today

G oing on the offense means hitting them as hard or harder than they hit you. Sometimes it means counter-attacking. Sometimes it means hitting them first.

By not just responding to accusations, corporations and individuals can challenge the credibility, the motives, even the decency of their accusers.

That political activist in the Northwest has long been an enemy of your industry. He's attacked other companies in the past and there's every reason to believe he will target you should a likely occasion arise. Let's see what kind of legitimate, related intelligence we can get on him now.

A media campaign based on offense would seem to be just one more item to add to the list of strategic options for companies and their advisors during crises. It is that, of course. In fact, it is often the first option to consider.

Yet, "offense" has a greater significance as well, directly related to many of the fundamental themes underlying public communications in our society today. As such, it is certainly an appropriate subject to conclude our book on media relations amid crisis and litigation.

Tactically, offense "introduces risk to your attackers," says Eric Dezenhall, President of Nichols Dezenhall, a crisis management firm in Washington, D.C. At the same time, it is an effort to *inoculate* a specific audience, perhaps a jury pool or consumer segment, with a specific message about the company or with its position on a key issue.

"Inoculate" is a precise usage here as well as a term of art. It denotes a process whereby serum is put into the public bloodstream so that future messages from the opposing camp—"germs," if you will —will be systemically rejected.

Most companies prefer the defensive. On the one hand, going on the offensive is uncomfortably reminiscent of the bad old days when corporations did go after their critics, but with altogether indefensible tactics, as when General Motors assigned a squadron of corporate goons to trail Ralph Nader and hopefully uncover compromising sexual behavior.

Yet in the larger sense, defensiveness is, at least these days, "in their DNA," as Richard Berman, President of Berman and Company, a communications firm in Washington, D.C., points out. Not that companies lack resources for an offense. What is publicity if not an offensive measure, only with positive, feel-good, self-promoting messages?

But transforming the corporate publicity machine into an attack mechanism is problematic, and often impossible, for a couple of reasons. First, the converting of one type of talent (for promotion) into another (for crisis management) requires effort. Whether the crisis calls for a defensive or an offensive strategy, it will demand a particular mindset that garden-variety publicists may presently lack.

Yet, there's a more basic reason why corporations remain in a defensive posture. To go on the offense often means taking not just a big risk, but also a very special kind of risk. On the one hand, capitalists take risks all the time. Risk management is part of doing business. They test new markets, invest in new products and sometimes they lose their money. In a crisis, smart capitalists often see, or can be taught to see, how the risks of not going on the offensive may clearly outweigh the risks of unleashing the Dobermans.

On the other hand, an offensive campaign can require a corporation to enter a socio-political fray where it will be taking sides, not just on specific issues, but in ongoing pitched battles between different segments of our society—plaintiffs in general versus corporate defendants in general, hawks versus doves, environmentalists versus energy producers, conservatives versus liberals, and so forth.

Corporations are in business to do business. They want to sell their products and make their shareholders happy. The status quo is their ideal. All this other stuff gets you onto an awfully slippery slope. No matter how they may personally feel about social issues, corporate executives are mighty uncomfortable siding with anyone in that ongoing 21st-century event known as the "culture wars."

Take a company like Coors Brewery. The great spurt in sales that Coors enjoyed occurred only after the public was lulled into forgetting the radical right-wing orientation of its founders, including opinions that had nothing to do with the labor squabbles in which the company was also involved. To maximize growth, to compete with Budweiser, you just can't limit your consumers to John Birch alumni.

Often, however, an industry's enemies are using or have even created a crisis specifically to score points in these culture wars. Rightly or wrongly, the products they're attacking, the corporate integrity they're questioning, are mere pretexts to propagate and reinforce their own larger agendas in the media and in the marketplace. The lawsuit against a hotel franchise we discussed in Chapter 2 was all about Muslim-American political aspirations, not the unfortunate experience of one hotel.

That being the case, a corporation may have no choice but to enter this fray. In some cases, going on the offensive guarantees that the company will, at some level, find itself engaged in a media-based debate on what the world itself ought to look like.

For a corporation, that is risky business to be sure. For the attorneys who help corporations respond to crises, the dangers of an offense require a summoning forth of all their skills and knowledge to help their clients stay on the safe side of libel. And, it means an all-the-more solid commitment on the part of attorneys to crisis planning and a guaranteed active role for them on the crisis team. Finally, it requires of attorneys a stern measure of self-transcendence, because attorneys—at least corporate attorneys—don't much like risk of any sort.

Here we are skirting the riskiest edge of public relations.

WHICH SIDE ARE YOU ON?

Corporations need only scrutinize the forces perennially arrayed against them to understand why there is often no way out of the culture wars. Berman describes the Non-Government Organizations (NGOs) as "institutional enemies…They are permanent enemies. They will never go away. Their agendas will never be satisfied. Environmental groups will always hate the lumber companies. The Naderites will always hate General Motors."

The impetus is not just money. The agenda is fundamentally iconoclastic, anti-corporate, and perhaps even revolutionary. On that kind of playing field, the choices for targeted industries are to fight back and swallow the bitter pill of socio-political entanglement when they'd rather just be selling products—or else surrender the field to resolute and often ruthless antagonists.

The enemy has many advantages that they will fully exploit if you don't go on the offense. For instance:

- NGOs, if not plaintiffs' attorneys, always start off with a better image than the companies they're attacking. They don't seem self-interested at all. They don't care about money. Corporations obviously do. "The ultimate weapon of the NGOs is credibility," says Berman.

- NGO public-spiritedness is underscored by their names. "People for the Ethical Treatment of All Living Things" sounds a lot more trustworthy than "Anaconda."

- They are driven by passion. Historically, passion tends to overthrow the empires built by greed. Staying on defense becomes tiresome. In this mode, companies feel less in control. They often suffer from "issue fatigue."

- The battle is "asymmetrical," says Berman, with the Davids on the NGO or plaintiffs' side fighting ceaseless guerilla war against corporate Goliaths. In this context, they can often self-justify illegal actions as the terrorists did on 9/11. (One assumes Berman is not quite so antipathetic to the illegal actions committed by the Norwegian underground in its "asymmetrical" posture toward the Nazis.) Less constraint provides them with decisive tactical advantages in some situations. It's their slingshot.

Scattershot counter-offensives are not enough. Once identified, potential enemies should be scrutinized on an ongoing basis. Maybe some NGO hasn't yet launched a specific offensive against your industry, but there's every reasonable prognostication that, in the fullness of time, it will do just that. Permanent surveillance is the only prophylactic response. Such ongoing surveillance by our corporate fathers may seem to have an Orwellian tinge but the NGOs are tax-exempt organizations feeding at the public trough. "Excellent research" and a passion for the "truth" are legitimate corporate weapons to keep these adversaries honest.

Corporations should be "watchdogs," using the media as messengers for their own interests and agendas. They have as much right to do so as Ralph Nader and the social justifications are often every bit as high-minded.

(Continued on page 197)

Anti-corporate Terrorism: A Daily Occurrence

Non-Government Organizations (NGOs) have decisive advantages in their sorties against global corporate capitalism. Passionate, agenda-driven warriors, they don't expect to win by simply arguing their cases in the media. The really radical ones know how to fight hard on many fronts. They know how to spot the soft underbelly. And they will utilize every weapon at their disposal to pierce it.

Consider one instance that shows just how formidable an NGO can be, and how a counter-offensive media strategy is both possible and sometimes necessary.

Huntingdon Life Sciences is a UK-based biosciences company with offices and investors throughout the United States. It does chemical testing on behalf of large companies and, since it uses animals in these tests, the company fell perilously afoul of an NGO called Stop Huntingdon Animal Cruelty (SHAC).

SHAC's tactic was to intimidate the employees, not of the company itself, but of its suppliers, actually going to people's homes and demanding that they pressure their employers to stop doing business with Huntingdon.

SHAC struck pay dirt with Marsh & McLennan, a major insurance company selling to Huntingdon. The insurer bowed to the pressure rather than invest a considerable sum in fighting back simply to support one small and, by its lights, insignificant customer.

The British government stepped in and eventually provided Huntingdon with insurance. But SHAC had sent a potent message to other NGOs: *This is how you can fight and win! This is how you should fight and win!* Meanwhile, as a parallel strategy, SHAC put so much pressure on investment firms Merrill Lynch and Charles Schwab that both companies eventually announced that they would no longer trade Huntingdon stock for investors. Other firms followed suit.

What might an anti-SHAC offense look like? Exposing

SHAC's methods is certainly a beginning but the strategic fulcrum is that SHAC's methods raise serious legal issues as well. *It is therefore as viable to make people afraid to associate with the organization as to make insurers and investment firms afraid to associate with Huntingdon.*

Sometimes the best counter-attack is a mirror image of the adversary's own strategy.

(*Continued from page 195*)

PICKING YOUR FIGHT

There is more art than science to media management during crises, and the decision to go on offense is no exception. One generally sound and rather obvious best practice is to take a hard look at your case. If it's a good case, then it's usually a good time to go on the offensive. If your adversaries are corrupt, or their position seriously mitigated by circumstance, sound the charge!

If it's a weak case, the better practice may be to develop your message points and then hunker down in the trenches. On the other hand, there are numerous instances when corporations or individuals will go on offense because it's simply the only thing they can do. (See Chapter 9 for discussion of defense versus offense options in regulatory matters.) By contrast, candid, defensive disclosures in response to negative coverage may create further legal exposure and possibly criminal or civil actions.

Apologies are often ineffective. Some common wisdom these days holds that Martha Stewart should have immediately apologized for what she did. Eric Dezenhall questions that wisdom. "Had Martha Stewart apologized, she would have been indicted in a nanosecond," he argues. Apologies are likewise ineffective when the charges against you involve a chronic pattern of malfeasance. "You can't apologize for twenty years in five minutes," advises Dezenhall.

People in such situations are cornered. But, if they may have no choice except attack, what should they actually tell the press?

The crucial criterion for your message, whether it's on the record or on deep background, is that it be related to the issue at hand. "Personal dirt is useless and sex will backfire," says Dezenhall. The important exception is when such behavior is, in fact, relevant to the charges flying back and forth. For example, conservatives preaching family values are fair game for exposure if they're cheating on their wives, says Dezenhall, a former media advisor in the Reagan White House.

The decision to launch a first attack, before the press gets hold of the story, also hinges on the case itself. Often, the purpose of the "inoculation" isn't so much to attack the adversary, but to prepare the media with message points that you know you'll need to use once the battle has begun—so why not use them now?

MAKE THE MESSENGER THE MESSAGE

In many instances, not only must the company choose sides in a war it would rather not fight, it must communicate in a way that is not always straightforward. The dynamics of crisis communications are not necessarily rational. In fact, the key component in offensive campaigns often involves "fogging the issue" (a term of art among the folks who do it for a living).

Fogging the issue means changing the story. To do so, you need to find an alternative—and legitimate—story that the press will jump at. In a classic offensive strategy, that alternative story is about the accuser: How the story is being developed, how and why information is being planted, how the media is being played. The media doesn't like being played and will aggressively turn against an accuser if they feel they've been manipulated. The purpose of an offense in that case may not necessarily be to harm or defame the adversary. The real purpose may be to simply bury their story by discrediting them with reporters.

Sometimes the media itself becomes the story if it has covered a case in a slanted way. It's a delicate media relations strategy, but the press does sometimes delight in self-laceration as a way to show how conscientious and thoughtful they are about their role in society. Your bad story doesn't go away altogether, but it could become the secondary story. The company can emerge as a sympathetic victim of media sloppiness or hysteria. Its products or executives may even be conspicuously exonerated as a result of such media *mea culpas*.

An option for Martha Stewart could have been for her to hammer home just how much overkill was going on in the press. Of course, there may never have really been a media solution available to Martha Stewart at any point, but making the press self-conscious about its own preoccupation was at least a tactical shot worth taking. When Rosie O'Donnell was taken to trial by her former publisher, she faced the cameras and said, "Dozens of Americans died last week in Iraq. Why am I on the front page?" The reporters got the message, and it certainly didn't hurt her case.

Many of the purported crisis management coups of recent years were really just celebrations of shrewd PR strategies; in other words, stories about the story. In some ways, there was nothing particularly remarkable about how Johnson & Johnson handled the Tylenol crisis, which is still a textbook example of expert crisis management. Everything the company did was pretty standard procedure, including the recall and, with a ready-made external villain (the psychopath tampering with their product), there was no question of corporate culpability at any point.

It was a no-brainer. Yet Johnson & Johnson created a story, in fact, a legend, all about its own public-spirited responsiveness.

There was no attack or offensive campaign in that situation as none was necessary. But the dynamic is instructively similar. You find an alternative story that will outlast and outshine the one you'd prefer to bury. Sometimes the alternative story is all about the accuser. Sometimes it's all about the messenger.

As long as it's not all about you!

So Don't Forget...

For corporations, going on offense is risky and repugnant. But your adversaries have dragged you into the fray whether you want to be there or not. As long as you're there...

- Identify your inevitable enemies. Often they're NGOs that have resolved to wage a permanent war against your industry. Go after them first. Expose their methods if those methods are reprehensible. Target their funding sources.

- Deliver your messages before you're asked. You know the sorts of defensive points you'll need to make once you're sued or attacked in the press. If you make those points now, before the fight has started, the media might very well believe them.

- Deflect unfavorable stories. By attacking your attackers, you create an alternative villain. By questioning the coverage itself, you may even make the media—not yourself—the centerpiece of media coverage.

- Make your attacks relevant to the issue. Sexual or other personal revelations will usually backfire. On the other hand, if they're calling you greedy, use any evidence you have of financial improprieties on their part, and use it for all it's worth.

Conclusion...Sort Of

The study of media relations during crises and during litigation can neither be conclusive nor comprehensive.

If real conclusiveness were possible, crises wouldn't be crises. They'd merely be situations that periodically arise and are successfully addressed by pressing a few time-tested buttons. Clearly, though, media management is part art and part science. When art is involved, there are always things left unsaid.

We've even advised in these pages that the best of best practices should, in certain instances, be jettisoned. Yes, "no comment" is almost always a bad practice, but "almost" is the operative word. There are times when you and your client should simply hide.

Comprehensiveness is equally impossible in the art of media management. Right now, Corporate America is suffering a protracted crisis that exploded first at Enron. This particular crisis has affected and, to one extent or another, changed how crisis managers understand their jobs. Next year, or the year after that, a new and equally critical, but very different, cultural event may loom large. It may require new rules, new approaches, and new best practices, or at least a rethinking of current practices.

Crisis means having to adapt to radical and unforeseen environmental changes. Mr. Darwin knew his stuff.

Even absent some sea change on the socio-political front, we cannot be comprehensive in our discussion. Many industries, like the tobacco industry or the automobile industry, face crises that are peculiar to their markets, and that require crisis managers to tailor very specific solutions. Addressing them all is well beyond our scope.

Let's conclude then, not with a final word, but with an invitation. Perhaps your industry grapples with unique media issues affected by fact patterns or marketplace variables that require separate treatment. Let us know. Let's explore those idiosyncratic exigencies in our next edition.

Litigation Planning Guide

When a lawsuit is filed against your company, two formidable tasks are at hand. First, you need a legal team and a legal strategy. That's what lawyers are for.

Second, you need a communications strategy—a multifaceted strategy that will encompass both your overall goals (what you want to say, how to protect the corporate brand, etc.) and a process by which to most effectively pursue those goals.

Here the communications strategy must be inextricably linked to the legal strategy and the case itself. Confronted with the myriad uncertainties ahead, how do you begin to get your hands around what you're going to say as well as when and to whom you're going to say it?

The template below is a planning guide to organize communications throughout the life of a lawsuit. It does not, and should not, dictate specific decisions. Instead, it creates a framework for making those decisions in a coherent and orderly fashion.

The planning guide also underscores a key aspect of all litigation PR and communications. Note that the action steps are geared to specific *milestones*: Notice of complaint, response to complaint, jury selection, opening statements, etc.

Litigation communications is based on such milestones for a number of reasons, the most salient of which is that each one is itself either a newsworthy story or a pretext to create a news story. As such, there's all likelihood that your adversary will seize on minor events to keep the story alive, and every milestone therefore needs to be included in the communications planning template.

This "Civil Action Communications Planner" was created by Alan Ulman, a corporate communications strategist based in Atlanta, Georgia. It is reproduced here with his permission.

CIVIL ACTION COMMUNICATIONS PLANNER	
Legal Procedure	**Communications Options**
1. Startup	A. Draft complaint-specific key messages and Q&A B. Set media protocol (i.e. response only or proactive) C. Identify and message-train spokesperson and third party influencers D. Identify and rate relevant media; advise legal team E. Draft holding statement that confirms commitment to customers, affirms our larger set of values, and questions plaintiff's standing
2. Notice of Complaint	*Consider statement to:* ☐ **Confirm recent receipt of notice** ☐ **Commit to properly reviewing and handling the matter** ☐ Confirm organizational commitment to core values and appropriate constituencies ☐ **Reserve further comment until review**
3. Complaint Filed/ Service of Complaint	*Consider statement to:* ☐ **Confirm recent receipt of complaint** ☐ **Commit to properly reviewing and handling the matter** ☐ Refute some or all allegations and counts ☐ Question the plaintiff's standing to file the complaint ☐ Confirm organizational commitment to core values and to constituencies ☐ **Reserve further comment until review**

CIVIL ACTION COMMUNICATIONS PLANNER	
Legal Procedure	**Communications Options**
4. Jurisdiction/ Venue/Judge	*Consider statement to:* ☐ **Express confidence in the jurisdiction/ venue/judge** ☐ Refute some or all allegations and counts ☐ Question the plaintiff's standing to file the complaint ☐ Confirm organizational commitment to core values and to ☐ **Express confidence in upcoming response to complaint**
5. Response to Complaint	*Consider statement to:* ☐ **Confirm and summarize filing of response to complaint** ☐ Refute some or all allegations and counts ☐ Question the plaintiff's standing to file the complaint ☐ Express confidence in the jurisdiction /venue/judge ☐ Confirm organizational commitment to core values and to constituencies ☐ **Express confidence in upcoming pre-trial motions**
6. Pre-Trial Motions	*Consider statement to:* ☐ **Confirm and summarize pre-trial motions** ☐ Refute some or all allegations and counts ☐ Question the plaintiff's standing to file the complaint ☐ Refute/invalidate plaintiff's pre-trial motions ☐ Confirm organizational commitment to core values and to constituencies ☐ **Express confidence in upcoming answer to complaint**

CIVIL ACTION COMMUNICATIONS PLANNER	
Legal Procedure	**Communications Options**
7. Answer to Complaint	*Consider statement to:* ☐ **Confirm and summarize answer to complaint** ☐ Refute some or all allegations and counts ☐ Express confidence in jurisdiction/venue/judge ☐ Confirm organizational commitment to core values and to constituencies ☐ **Express confidence in upcoming discovery**
8. Discovery	*Consider statement to:* ☐ **Express confidence based on discovery** ☐ **Express confidence in our findings; question the plaintiff's findings** ☐ **Establish our third parties; refute/invalidate the plaintiff's third parties** ☐ Confirm and summarize answer to complaint/ refute some or all allegations and counts ☐ Confirm organizational commitment to core values and to constituencies ☐ **Express confidence in upcoming jury selection**
9. Pre-Trial Conference	*Consider statement to:* ☐ **Express confidence based outcome of pre-trial conference** ☐ Confirm and summarize answer to complaint/ refute some or all allegations and counts ☐ Confirm confidence in discovery and our third parties/refute/invalidate plaintiff's discovery and third parties ☐ Confirm organizational commitment to core values and to constituencies ☐ **Express confidence in upcoming jury selection**

CIVIL ACTION COMMUNICATIONS PLANNER	
Legal Procedure	**Communications Options**
10. Jury Selection	*Consider statement to:* ☐ **Express confidence in jury/jury pool** ☐ Confirm and summarize answer to complaint/ refute some or all allegations and counts ☐ Confirm confidence in discovery and our third parties/refute/invalidate plaintiff's discovery and third parties ☐ Confirm organizational commitment to core values and to constituencies ☐ **Express confidence in upcoming opening statements**
11. Opening Statements	*Consider statement to:* ☐ **Question merits of plaintiff statement** ☐ **Highlight defense statement** ☐ Confirm confidence in our third parties/refute/ invalidate plaintiff's third parties ☐ Express confidence in court, jury ☐ Confirm organizational commitment to core values and to constituencies ☐ **Set up statement to refute/invalidate upcoming plaintiff's case**
12. Plaintiff's Case	*Consider statement to:* ☐ **Question merits of plaintiff case** ☐ Refute/invalidate plaintiff's third parties ☐ Express confidence in court, jury ☐ Confirm organizational commitment to core values and to constituencies ☐ **Set up statement for upcoming motion for directed verdict**

CIVIL ACTION COMMUNICATIONS PLANNER	
Legal Procedure	**Communications Options**
13. Motion for Directed Verdict	*Consider statement to:* ☐ **Make the case for a directed verdict** ☐ Question the merits of plaintiff case ☐ Refute/invalidate plaintiff's third parties ☐ Express confidence in court ☐ Confirm organizational commitment to core values and to constituencies ☐ **Set up statement on upcoming defense case**
14. Defendant's Case	*Consider statement to:* ☐ **Highlight defense case** ☐ **Refute/invalidate plaintiff's cross examination** ☐ Express confidence in court, jury ☐ Confirm organizational commitment to core values and to constituencies ☐ **Set up statement to refute/invalidate upcoming plaintiff's rebuttal**
15. Plaintiff's Rebuttal/ Answer to Plaintiff's Rebuttal	*Consider statement to:* ☐ **Refute/invalidate plaintiff's rebuttal** ☐ **Highlight answer to plaintiff's rebuttal** ☐ Express confidence in court, jury ☐ Confirm organizational commitment to core values and to constituencies ☐ **Set up statement on closing arguments**

CIVIL ACTION COMMUNICATIONS PLANNER	
Legal Procedure	**Communications Options**
16. Closing Arguments	*Consider statement to:* ☐ **Highlight defense argument** ☐ **Refute/invalidate plaintiff's argument** ☐ Express confidence in court, jury ☐ Confirm organizational commitment to core values and to constituencies ☐ **Set up statement on jury instructions**
17. Jury Instructions	*Consider statement to:* ☐ **Highlight defense argument** ☐ **Refute/invalidate plaintiff's argument** ☐ Express confidence in court, jury ☐ Confirm organizational commitment to core values and to constituencies ☐ **Set up statement on jury instructions**
18. Verdict	*Consider statement to:* ☐ **Express gratitude for not guilty verdict –or–** ☐ **Express disappointment in guilty verdict and set up appeal** ☐ Confirm organizational commitment to core values and to constituencies ☐ **If found guilty set up statement on judgment and execution**
19. Judgment & Execution	*Consider statement to:* ☐ **Express disappointment in guilty verdict and set up appeal** ☐ Confirm organizational commitment to core values and to constituencies

A Crisis Management Primer for In-House Counsel

Crisis and media management represents not just an ancillary service provided by law firms, but a critical component of case strategy in litigation practice. Crisis management is a two-way street, a partnership between inside and outside counsel to which law firms, drawing on diverse client representations, can sometimes apply invaluable battle-tested experience.

A few years ago, Michael Wagner, a partner and litigator at Baker & McKenzie in Chicago, as well as a former journalist, prepared a primer for clients that neatly sums up, and adds to, many of the best practices enumerated in this book. The guidelines are presented in unabridged form.

Minimizing Legal Risk While Managing the Corporate Crisis: A Primer with Proactive Strategies and Practical Suggestions

©2003 Michael J. Wagner

1) The Importance of Preparing a Crisis Management Plan and Assembling the Team

a) Why Are Proactive Plans Necessary?

The legal risks and financial stakes are simply too high. Corporations can no longer afford to be reactive rather than proactive.

  i) If your company is aware of a problem and fails to address it, it could face the specter of punitive damages in many states.

  ii) Remember those who failed—and learn from their experience.

b) Members of the Team

  i) Senior management
    (1) CEO preferred
    (2) CFO also should be involved, both for financial and for securities disclosure implications.
    (3) General Counsel—the team's quarterback
    (4) Key vice presidents
      (a) Human Resources—to ensure appropriate, accurate information flow to your employees
      (b) Sales and Marketing—to gauge customers' response and keep them in the information loop at a critical time
      (c) Risk Management—to deal with insurers and address potential liability concerns with General Counsel and outside counsel

  ii) Outside counsel
    (1) Agile SWAT team approach

(a) interviewing witnesses

(b) retaining consultants

(c) preserving work product and attorney-client privileges

(d) interacting with regulatory authorities (e.g., state, local and federal public health agencies, EPA, OSHA, USDA, FDA)

(2) Absolutely essential where litigation is anticipated or inevitable

iii) First-rate public relations counsel

iv) Risk manager—May be in-house or outside firm

2) Reducing Liability Risk and Damages Exposure: Implementing the Plan and Mobilizing the Team

a) Speak With One Corporate Voice

i) Remember the Six Cs:

(1) Concerned

(2) Clear

(3) Consistent

(4) Credible

(5) Concise

(6) Compassionate, especially in the case of a catastrophe

ii) The importance of consistency cannot be overestimated

(1) Closing the loop of communication is critical.

(2) Inconsistent comments by company employees and middle managers in different locations can create major liability problems—especially in areas such as quality assurance, corporate compliance and risk management ("We maintain the highest standards" versus "Sometimes things fall through the cracks") and government regulatory compliance ("We adhere closely to govern-

ment standards" versus "We do the best we can, but sometimes the red tape is too much to bear …").

iii) Clarity enhances credibility

iv) "No comment" is no help—and often hurts

    (1) Presumption of guilt: Survey data shows consumers/ public believe companies that do not comment are guilty, hiding something, or otherwise responsible.

    (2) A missed opportunity to earn trust with key stakeholders: Customers, shareholders, public, media (both general and financial), regulators, lenders and creditors

b) Have the Team—and Especially Outside Counsel— "On Call"

  i) General counsel or other designated corporate liaison in charge of disaster planning is the "hub of the wheel," coordinating communications to ensure a consistent prompt response and minimize liability exposure.

  ii) Home, office and cell phone numbers of all team members, especially chief outside counsel, should be on your Blackberry, your speed-dial, your Contacts directory, your Rolodex and at your fingertips.

c) Once the Crisis Hits, Outside Counsel and the Designated Corporate Liasion Should Mobilize and Meet As Soon As Possible

  i) Interviewing key witnesses and/or participants to ascertain what happened—and how to keep it from happening again

  ii) Working with—and reassuring—the appropriate regulatory authorities.

  iii) Retaining consultants and industry experts can help companies chart the correct course early—to get at the root of the perceived problem or media target area, to reassure regulatory authorities, and to suggest appropriate proactive strategic responses (e.g., revamp or reaffirm GMP and product safety protocols, evaluate food preparation policies, reassess corporate compliance programs).

   (1) Government or former government officials should be involved wherever possible.

      (a) wrapping the company in the mantle of regulatory credibility

      (b) avoid the "shill syndrome"

iv) Multi-jurisdictional crises require multi-jurisdictional responses.

   (1) For problems that arise in more than one forum, an outside counsel firm with a national or, better yet, international presence and substantial resources, is often in the best position to respond in each venue, if necessary.

v) Protecting and preserving legal privileges

   (1) Attorney-client work product privileges may vary widely from state to state, so familiarizing yourself with the scope of protections afforded in the state(s) at issue is essential.

   (2) Witness statements or consultant findings that fall within a broad blanket work product protection in some states, or in federal court, may be automatically discoverable in other jurisdictions.

   (3) Beware of PR privilege pitfalls: Though the recent case law trend is encouraging, no bright line test or road map has emerged yet

d) Don't Get Hoisted on Your Petard: Avoiding the Careless Email and Paper Trails

   i) Especially important when dealing with groups presenting potentially high litigation risks (e.g., sales representatives, R&D, Quality Assurance)

   ii) Educating staff through internal training.

   (1) Counsel should advise employees that what they say in

writing could follow them around long after they leave the company or even retire.

(2) A healthy perspective: How would this look in litigation?

iii) Explore whether any renegade or disgruntled employees are playing a role in the problem.

(1) Let staff know that a "boys will be boys" mentality will not be tolerated.

iv) Evaluate whether the local or regional manager is well-respected by the rank-and-file—to ensure that reliable information is getting to the top.

v) Ensure that the key decision-makers have direct contact with those in the center of the storm.

e) Ambush Prevention Strategies

i) To avoid liability problems and ensure a consistent response, place "friendly reminder" emails and faxes near key points of contact with the media or other constituency.

(1) Locations: Phone, cashier, receptionist, local manager's office

(2) Advise staff who the designated corporate voice is.

(3) Let those located in the likely line of media contact know what to do when the media onslaught comes.

ii) Rapid communication is the key, since every plant, facility, store, outlet or restaurant becomes a potential target even if only one of them is facing a crisis.

f) If You Are Planning to Take Statements, Conduct Tests, or Make Findings, If At All Possible, Do Not Reduce Them to

Writing Until You Have Good Reason to Believe the Results Will Be Favorable or Supportive.

    i) Especially important in litigation-prone areas

    ii) Why create unfavorable evidence for your opponent's closing argument to the jury? ("Don't take my word for it. The defendant generated it.")

    iii) Exception: Some regulatory requirements and agencies may limit your options and leave you little choice.

3) The Absolute Importance Of Becoming A Non-Story—And Getting Off The Nightly News

a) Remember There are Two Courts About Which to be Concerned—The Court of Public Opinion and the Court of Law.

b) The Longer Your Crisis Attracts Media Attention, the More Likely Inconsistent Statements—And Potential Liability Problems—Will Arise.

c) If Liability Looks Likely (and Even in Some Cases Where It Does Not but Your Losses in the Court Of Public Opinion Look Sufficiently Daunting), Do Your Best to Settle Soon, Settle Quietly, and Settle Confidentially.

    i) Verify that the state where the problem arose will permit confidentiality agreements.

    ii) Even in those states less likely to enforce confidentiality agreements, seek to obtain confidentiality anyway.

    iii) Advise management and/or the appointed "point person" about the importance of avoiding admissions in conversations with claimants and potential plaintiffs.

iv) Customize settlement releases for the precise complaint or series of complaints; bring your laptop to the site to tailor the document quickly, according to the exigencies of the particular situation.

v) Preparing the media release and public statement

(1) Above all else, demonstrate concern.

(2) Correctly framing the issue is critical.

(3) Describe what steps your company has already taken— and what steps it plans to take—to resolve the crisis.

(4) Work closely with other team members, especially in-house/outside counsel and public relations consultant, in crafting the final draft.

d) Beware of Winning the Liability Battle, Only To Lose the Sales War

Crisis Scenarios

Below we've included a number of fictional crisis scenarios. They are practical tools for readers to reflect on how they'd react in such exigent situations. Hopefully, your PR and legal teams can make direct use of the scenarios for role-playing and training exercises, whatever the nature of your business or the particular kind of crisis you may someday encounter.

I. Product Liability: Reassuring the Public, Protecting an Investment

You are the in-house general counsel of The Tick-Tock Watch Company. The company has just brought out an illumination product called EverGlo that is the first of its kind in the market. Simply touch the watch and the watch face glows. EverGlo was launched just in time for Christmas, 2006. It is projected to represent 20 percent of Tick-Tock's total global revenue in 2007, and likely more in the coming years.

Last week, Tick-Tock's environmental compliance officer informed the General Counsel that a routine check of the company's Peoria headquarters, where the watches are manufactured, revealed an abnormal concentration of CS-511, a low-level toxin. A residue of CS-511 was used in an industrial cleaning solvent by Tick-Tock three decades ago.

As the low levels of toxin were found on the edge of the Tick-Tock property—a sprawling suburban landscape of a few hundred acres—the toxin may not be present as a result of Tick-Tock's use. The neighboring community has been there as long as the Tick-Tock headquarters and CS-511 had been commonly found in some household cleaning products years ago.

Both the U.S. Environmental Protection Agency and the Illinois EPA have been notified, with the state agency taking the lead in the investigation. The regulators are not interested in divulging information to the press and they appreciate Tick-Tock's assiduous self-reporting of the matter. Unfortunately, the press has picked up the rumors anyway.

The press is also well aware of how, 60 years ago, radium had been used in the manufacture of watch dials, which allowed them to be read in the dark. As a result of the radium, a number of Tick-Tock's employees (mainly female) developed tongue cancer from licking the brushes to make the tips fine enough for painting dials. It became an industry-wide problem but, as one of the largest watch dial manufacturers in the United States, Tick-Tock is the company remembered for it.

A few minutes ago, Tick-Tock's in-house press officer, who only handles product public relations, informed you that the local daily newspaper called for a statement. It was the lead business reporter who usually gets his stories on the front page of the paper. Worse, his stories, when they include national angles, are occasionally picked up by the wire services and run in major dailies around the country.

If the story goes on for too many days, calls are likely to come in from other major newspapers in the state as Tick-Tock is one of the largest employers in the Peoria region.

Local coverage is likely to be fair, but nonetheless critical. The more negative, the more likely the story will get picked up by other papers. Restricting the story to local coverage would be considered a victory, since it would then be less likely to have much, if any, impact on Tick-Tock.

No prepared statement is ready. The Peoria reporter is expecting a call back from a Tick-Tock spokesperson within three hours. As GC, you call your outside counsel. After a discussion of the legal issues, you ask for media advice.

- Does the company return the reporter's call?

- If so, who should the spokesperson be?

- What should the focus of the conversation be?

- Are there any ground rules you want to set?

- Should you prepare a statement?

- What should the statement say?

- Do you acknowledge responsibility?

- What should your overall media strategy be?

- What questions should you ask?

Once you have answered these questions, prepare for the actual live interview.

II. Reputation or Litigation: Weighing Opposing Risks

The CEO wants to see you in 15 minutes about a legal matter that may be in *The Wall Street Journal* tomorrow. You, the chief legal officer of Hartwell Department Stores—a publicly traded retail giant with 1,000 stores in North America—walk into a large conference room to find the CEO with a tense look in his eyes. Beside him sits the public relations director and the heads of marketing and product lines, all with nervous expressions on their faces.

The CEO reminds everyone that, not too long ago, the company entered into an exclusive agreement with Benicia, an upscale design company, to supply goods. Everyone at Hartwell considered the deal a great coup and expected increased sales from the arrangement. A multi-million dollar contract was signed, the initial shipments of the goods were delivered, and, indeed, Hartwell happily watched its sales dramatically increase.

This deal was only the latest in a series of shrewd moves by Hartwell involving Benicia. Just five years ago, Hartwell was a largely blue-collar-based business. As Hartwell picked up Benicia lines, it successfully changed its image to reach middle-class and upscale customers as well. The recent agreement on exclusive distributorship caps this strategy.

Hartwell's customer base now cuts across class lines. The alliance with Benicia is an important business relationship, to be sure.

But in the past several weeks, Benicia has received negative press over a number of its ads that are offensive to Hartwell's essentially conservative core customer base. Some of the ads are overtly sexual. Others are insensitive to handicapped people. By association, the public outcry has spilled over to Hartwell. The head of PR tried to disassociate the company from the bad press by issuing press releases but, so far, the effort has failed.

Hartwell had warned Benicia about the ads before the bad press began. In fact, there's a paper trail, including letters to Benicia from Hartwell executives, as well as memoranda summarizing meetings in which those warnings were repeated.

The CEO looks around the table. "Any ideas what to do?" he asks.

There's no easy answer: If you terminate the contract, you'll violate the agreement and open up the company to a lawsuit. But if you honor the contract, the company's reputation will continue to be attacked. Meanwhile, sales of Benicia products by Hartwell have dropped 40% since the bad press began.

Essentially, the task is to evaluate two different types of risk.

Is there a middle ground that the company can find where it can quell the public disapproval and still honor its contract?

If so, what is the message? How is the message to be delivered?

If not, which alternative risk is worth taking? What is the worst-case scenario in taking the reputational risk? What are the advantages in doing so?

What is the worst-case scenario in taking the legal risk? What are the advantages in doing so?

What information does the company need, and what information do you need, to render an informed judgment?

Can the letters and memoranda expressing Hartwell's past concerns about the ads be used now to help Hartwell, either legally or in the press?

How fast can a decision be made? Fast enough for tomorrow's *Wall Street Journal*? If not, is there a "holding statement" you can issue that will satisfy the reporter for now, without undermining the further statement you will make once a decision is made?

The CEO needs to leave this meeting armed with both a general strategic plan as to what kind of risk Hartwell will run as well as specific action points to implement the strategy.

III. The Cross-Border Factor: Corporate Crisis amid Political Crisis

The Paris-based LeFlore Corp. has just suffered major economic reversals in two of its most important divisions: in-flight food services (the Regale division) and a large food import/export division (the Appetite division). LeFlore must reduce force worldwide and may even close the Regale division altogether, as it has never really recovered from 9/11.

Hardest hit are 500 Regale employees on both U.S. coasts as well as 100 Appetite employees in California. Around 100 employees in Europe are also facing termination. These European positions are scattered throughout various LeFlore divisions.

On May 1, LeFlore announces that the first round of layoffs will begin on July 1 in both the United States and Europe. There is no accompanying statement as to the economic condition of the company nor reference to the future viability of any particular division.

On May 10, the California city where Regale has its U.S. headquarters files suit, claiming breach of promise. LeFlore had made a

10-year commitment to the city when it first negotiated its U.S. site, although the language of that written commitment is fairly vague. The following day, three women in an upstate New York town where Appetite has a service division file separate suits, each claiming sexual harassment by a supervisor (who is American).

As senior U.S. in-house counsel for LeFlore, you have been advised by Paris to take charge of the litigation. You are well aware of the economic realities (including the possibility that Regale might have to dissolve), and you are also aware that anti-French sentiment has been percolating because of the Iraqi war.

Calls from local reporters in California and upstate New York have poured into the corporate press office, most of them just after the layoff announcement and before the filings of the lawsuits in New York. None of the calls were answered. There is no additional statement beyond the original announcement. And no message points are prepared. You're working with an empty slate.

Now comes a worst-case scenario: the head of LeFlore's communications department advises that *The New York Times* has picked up the story. While *The Times* reporter may himself be above French-bashing, the fact that LeFlore's announcement has caused intense community response on both coasts is newsworthy. Anti-French hostility is the subject and LeFlore the poster boy.

The Times reporter wants an interview now (Wednesday) for the Friday edition. He will likely ask you to comment on the anti-French feelings. He will also ask about the company's situation and why the layoffs are necessary. He may or may not ask about the merits of the lawsuits. There is a strong likelihood that more newspapers in major markets will subsequently cover the story as well, including the tabloids.

There are any number of vital points that must be covered with your legal and PR advisors:

- Should you talk to *The Times* reporter? Should you now talk to any or all of the local newspapers that called?

- Should you be the spokesperson or should an outside advisor talk to the press?

- What comment if any about U.S.-French relations would serve the company's interests? What kind of public statements might insulate LeFlore from the political situation?

- What kind of public statements might defuse local tensions?

- Can you, or should you, disclose just how dire Regale's situation is and that it might close altogether if drastic steps aren't taken?

- To what extent can you address the specifics of the suits by the city in California and by the female employees in upstate New York?

- Can you comment on the disproportionate number of layoffs in the United States?

While you're on the phone with your outside legal and PR advisors, your communications director chats with *The Times* reporter and wins a delay until next morning. You've no choice but to do the interview, but you do have a little more breathing room to prepare.

IV. Media Terror: Protecting Reputation during a National Panic

In 2001, the Al-Jeddah Bank, based in Saudi Arabia, earmarked $6 billion in equity for diverse U.S. investment. By 2008, it will have taken strong positions in major urban real estate developments, with a half-dozen separate limited partnerships coast to coast. The bank is working closely with a number of Americans.

Six months later, Al-Qaeda attacks New York and Washington. Six years later, flamboyant plaintiff's counsel Todd Morris sues more than a dozen Middle Eastern financial institutions, including Al-Jeddah, for allegedly funneling money to terrorists.

A blanket denial has already been issued but there have been no personal responses to media inquiries in either the United States or the United Kingdom. No strategy has been developed since the suit was filed.

A major network investigative reporter has contacted the bank's office in Paris where Al-Jeddah's president has been conferring with his advisor. In a brief message, the reporter informed the bank that Morris claims to have decisive evidence of a sizable wire transfer.

Morris fashions himself a social crusader and is probably not interested in a settlement. Any defeat for Al-Jeddah in court may mean literally thousands of derivative suits. Any negative press coverage can torpedo its U.S. projects. It is essential to send messages that will reassure the bank's American partners, at least enough to keep them from bolting the various projects.

Total potential exposure is clearly in the billions.

Al-Jeddah's president wants to know what else he can do besides maintaining innocence in the U.S. and UK media. And, he wants to know what surprises might be in store from the media.

V. Health Care: Sending the Right Message

Last week a class action suit was filed against Bankable Health Provision, a large national HMO, for refusal to reimburse Viagra prescriptions over a stipulated cost threshold. In making the decision, the company was taking a calculated risk. As CEO, you are fully aware that there are contractual issues that will likely engender high-volume litigation. That liability was weighed against the skyrocketing costs of Viagra. The decision was made to go forward with the reimbursement limits.

Working with an outside PR firm, a strong "message point" was developed that maintains the HMO's right to set arbitrary but reasonable limits and makes the additional argument that a prescription for any drug, in the face of untenable volume, is subject to such limits by all insurers.

Enough Viagra reimbursement cases have been dismissed in recent months to reassure Bankable Health that the litigation risks and exposures are acceptable.

This morning, however, a bombshell exploded. Bankable Health Senior VP Louis Lipp talked out of school to *The Chicago Tribune*. He is quoted as saying: (1) Too many people are using Viagra recreationally, not just as a treatment for impotence; (2) Too many doctors are prescribing Viagra without sufficient medical cause; (3) A drug like Viagra will bankrupt the health insurance industry; and (4) We shouldn't be paying out claims just so people can have sex every night.

The headline in the paper is "HMO Giant on Viagra Counterattack." Pfizer, the manufacturer, refused to comment for the story. But one Big Pharma spokesperson is quoted, depicting Bankable Health's position as "unsustainable" while further suggesting "there are a number of health insurers in this country who are probably in the wrong business."

You'll deal with Mr. Lipp later. Right now you have to deal with two newswires and four other national newspapers ready and able to portray Bankable Health as a company that takes an antagonistic view toward Viagra in general, and, judging from Mr. Lipp, one that maintains strong views about whether such a drug should even be prescribed.

Your PR advisor and general counsel hurry to your office. The task is to determine:

- What damage has Lipp's comments done both to your litigation/business strategy and to your reputation?

- Should you proactively launch a media campaign to clarify the company's position or hope the story dies down before the depositions begin?

- What do you say to the press right now?

- Do you still pursue your strategy to limit reimbursements?

- Do you change your central message point?

- Should you disassociate yourself from Lipp? If so, when and how?

- Do you call Pfizer for any reason?

More is at risk than just the class action suit that's already been filed. Defeat in the media and in the courts can mean lasting damage to the company's reputation while you wind up paying the claims anyway.

VI. Big Pharma: Disadvantaging the Handicapped

MartinJackson Inc. has aggressively cut shipments of its arthritis drug Vigorate to Canada since thousands of Americans are paying 30% to 50% percent less by ordering the drug on the Internet. Two related developments spell trouble. First, the leading senior citizen advocacy groups have denounced MaritinJackson's move in the press and are promising retaliation in the form of protests and boycotts.

Second, a leading competitor has proactively informed the world that it will not decrease shipments of its arthritis drug to Canada because, according to a press release, "we do not choose to interfere with the rights of arthritis patients, young and old, to find the best prescription drug solutions for themselves."

MartinJackson has also just launched a multi-million dollar TV campaign to market Vigorate, guaranteeing that the negative story will be refreshed in people's minds whenever they see the commercials.

A full-page ad in *The New York Times* underscores how organized are the forces confronting MartinJackson. The groups include online pharmacies, senior citizen groups, and patient advocates. The ad says, "MartinJackson is taking away the right of arthritis victims to affordable prescription drugs." The media frenzy has already begun. The newswires and the morning television shows are particular danger zones.

MartinJackson's first response had been a public service announcement claiming that buying drugs over the Internet is not safe. The tactic backfired. The message was scoffed at, and begged the question, "Why don't you sell the drug to us at a reasonable price in a safer venue?"

The CEO has informed the board that its decision to cut shipments is non-negotiable.

The tasks at hand:

- Decide if the company wants to proactively defend its actions or accept a few bad press days, hoping the hubbub will subside.

- Identify a spokesperson(s) to counteract accusations from elderly "victims" of the company's imputed callousness. Should the company rely on its own articulate C-suite spokespersons, especially the dynamic CEO, or tap outside supporters for public commentary? If so, who should those spokespersons be and what should they say?

- In general, what message points are now required? Should they address the specific situation and the business necessity of cutting Canadian shipments? Should they go beyond the specific situation and stress the social value of the company's other products and its valuable research contributions?

- How can you argue "business necessity" when your competitors are not cutting shipments to Canada?

- What lesson do you draw from the failure of the public service announcement about the safety of buying drugs on the Internet?

- What sort of specific responses to imminent events, especially protest marches and boycotts, are advisable? Is there a single message point to address all such events, or should the company be prepared to reformulate its message with each new sortie by the opposition?

- Do you pull or change your current marketing campaign for Vigorate?

- What role, if any, might an alternative advertising or public service campaign play?

- What role, if any, might a company-sponsored philanthropic initiative play?

Congress will be taking up the issue later this year, so the stakes are sky-high. Not only is your immediate competitive position in jeopardy, but a political setback on the Hill might permanently put you at the mercy of Canada-based suppliers underselling your retail prescriptions to millions of customers.

VII. A Law Firm in Trouble: Controlling the Story

1. It's Monday morning and John Parsons, the managing partner of Burns & Beltvay, a well-known Washington, D.C. law firm, has just received word that the entire government contracts practice group will be moving to a competitor firm. There are 12 letters of resignation on his desk, five from partners and seven from associates. While the ink is still fresh on the letters, a call from an *American Lawyer* reporter lands on Parsons' voice mail.

Parsons doesn't know how many of his other partners are aware of what has happened, although relations between the executive committee and the government contracts lawyers had been conspicuously strained for months. In some ways, their departure is not altogether negative, as the most profitable practices by far are the fairly new corporate and biotech groups that have prospered despite the tech downturn. It's a chance to really clean shop and drive firm-wide profits higher.

The possibilities confronting the firm are thus either very positive or, if the wrong messages are sent, very negative. There are a few complications as well, including low associate satisfaction rankings and a London office (also corporate) that has been hemorrhaging money. It's a firm in transition, with strong liabilities and assets in its current position.

The *American Lawyer* interview is crucial. It will set the tone for any other interview on the subject. *AmLaw's* sister publications will likely pick up Parsons' comments as well, especially in Texas and Florida where the firm has handled high-profile matters. If the U.K. press pays attention, they'll pounce hard and focus particularly on the faltering London office (which has so far escaped the local media radar screen).

Challenge: Evolve the right message point. Make it sound believable. Assuage the other partners.

2. Parsons finishes the *American Lawyer* interview around 2 pm. At 3 pm, he meets Joe Farrell, head of the firm's small employment practice, in the coffee room. "Oh by the way," says Farrell, "some guy from *The Washington Post* called me about DimStar." DimStar is a major biotech company based in Maryland that the firm helped grow from a start-up. "I guess that complaint against Thompson has gotten out."

Parsons is appalled. A DimStar secretary had filed suit against DimStar and CFO Jack Thompson for sexual harassment. Farrell fears that, if the press has picked up on it, they will piggyback the story on a year-old harassment charge against a partner in the firm.

That case was settled quietly. Fortunately, it was more or less ignored at the time by the legal press. Unfortunately, it did receive a little ink and was posted on legal news websites. Anyone covering the DimStar situation might well stumble on it. The accused partner is still with Burns & Beltvay and has handled transactions for DimStar.

For an enterprising reporter, there's a real feature on the firm lurking in the wings. Such a feature would portray an out-of-control partnership that is harassing secretaries, losing lawyers in droves, torturing associates, and wasting money on ill-advised transatlantic ventures.

Taken in pieces, each component is explainable. Taken as a whole, it's a damaging portrait and the DimStar harassment problem is just the spark to ignite a firm-wide fire, even though the complaint against Jack Thompson actually happened someplace else.

It is therefore imperative that Burns & Beltvay help DimStar manage the Thompson media crisis as effectively as possible, not only as a matter of client service but of direct self-interest as well. Choice of spokesperson to respond to the media on behalf of DimStar is crucial. So are the message points. So are the responses to any reporter who may ask about the year-old sex complaint against Burns & Beltvay, or even mention it casually.

Challenge: Help Farrell and DimStar manage the media in a way that minimizes the story. Prepare for the worst if the old allegation against Burns & Beltvay is revived. Fragment the Burns & Beltvay story to discourage reporters from piecing together these various discrete problems into one damning whole.

VIII. A Celebrity Client: The Guy They Love to Hate

Joe Walker, one of the most arrogant and widely disliked, but perennially high-scoring, stars in the National Basketball Association, is arrested for assault and battery. The victim is in a coma. The evidence against Walker is strong but not conclusive. Walker's lawyer has made a predictable assertion of innocence on the courtroom steps.

Reporters are clamoring to talk to Walker and his lawyer naturally counsels his client not to give any interviews. But Walker has already told one sports reporter that his victim was "just a jerk."

Reporters are also clamoring to talk to Susan Farrell, Walker's agent.

Farrell is very worried. Walker's team is not a playoff contender, so the PR liabilities of keeping Walker on the roster could outweigh any benefits of letting him play. There is a morals clause in Walker's contract. If there is enough public outrage, the team might well exercise it. That would be bad news for Farrell since her stake is 15 percent of $20 million.

Farrell is convinced that someone besides Walker's lawyer ought to talk to the press as daily coverage has been rehashing past misdeeds. Farrell herself is a former publicist and well liked by sports writers. She also attracts a lot of media attention on her own, having been the first woman agent to represent athletes at this level.

Farrell decides to grant an interview. After all, she might as well. With a few more days of bad press, Walker could be out of a job and Farrell out of a commission. But first she needs to get a few message points in line. She's also wondering if it might actually be beneficial to do a joint press interview with Walker, despite his lawyer's prohibition.

Suddenly her secretary rings. Two old friends from the *Post Gazette* would like to see her. She decides to see them and talk about Walker.

Her audience is the public and also the team management. Her goal is to save Walker's job, at least until the case is decided in court. Or until her commission check clears.

What should she say?